HEALING POWER OF MEDITATION

WISDOM AND ENCOURAGEMENT FROM THE
MEDITATION CENTER OF ALABAMA

LAR NIMIT M.A CPA

PHRA NICHOLAS THANISSARO PH.D.

CAY WELSH PH.D.   KENT WELSH PH.D.

SERENA NIMITYONGSKUL M.D.

JENNIFER A. BRANTLEY M.S.   FORREST NEAL

Illustrated by BOBBY BARNHILL

Edited by TAYLOR KELLIHER

Edited by JENNIFER A. BRANTLEY

LAKEVIEW
PUBLICATIONS

Bulk order information

Happiness072@gmail.com

If you would like an emailed list for meditation classes and retreats, please reach out to us at:

www.meditationcenteral.com

Published: LakeView Publications
Formatting: Craig A. Price
Cover Design: Bobby Barnhill
Edited: Taylor Kelliher & Jennifer A. Brantley

This book is dedicated to the life and teachings of Mr. Robert (Bob) Mawson, who became the first European ever certified to teach Dhammakāya meditation as a lay instructor. Mr. Mawson was instrumental in establishing the Meditation Center of Alabama in Mobile and was the first to teach weekly meditation classes. Mr. Mawson's tireless efforts allowed the Center to develop and grow a following of students and supporters that continues to flourish today.

Special Thanks to our contributing authors:

Phra Nicholas Thanissaro Ph.D.
Cay Welsh Ph.D.
Kent Welsh Ph.D.
Serena Nimityongskul M.D.
Jennifer A. Brantley M.S.
Forrest Neal

PREFACE

This book chronicles the story of one person's quest to change the world for the better. My mother, Lar Nimit, began meditating many years ago and discovered that true peace and happiness actually lies within the mind, through peace and acceptance of reality. After discovering this powerful truth she began her quest to share her knowledge and tool for ultimate peace with the world. She founded a non- profit organization, The Meditation Center of Alabama, in 2007. Since then she has been sued for "illegal meditation" retreats at her house, publicly discriminated against, and fought for the right to help others on a community and legal scale. Her rise to overcome and persevere despite all obstacles has been the greatest example of never giving up and fighting for the right to help others that I have ever seen in my life.

Through her dedication and unwavering belief in the goodness of the mission she has for the world she has successfully built the Meditation Center of Alabama to what it is today, a thriving community of peace seekers who regard each other as family, a community of peace leaders actively teaching, sharing and volunteering their time to brings acts of peace and kindness to the world. To bring the peace off the mat, starting from ourselves, one person at a time, with patience, compassion and understanding until world peace is finally attained through each individual person's attainment of true, lasting and personal peace. This is her story and gift to the world.

FIGHTING FOR THE RIGHT TO HELP OTHERS

MY STORY OF THE MEDITATION CENTER OF ALABAMA

LAR NIMIT, M.A., CPA, FOUNDER

I was born and raised in Thailand and am the youngest of twelve siblings. On the weekend, my parents occasionally took our family to the Buddhist temple where we chanted, prayed, and offered food to the monks. At the time, I did not know the meanings of those activities or how to meditate, since the temple that we went to focused primarily on chanting and prayer.

In Thailand, there are thousands of Buddhist temples. Some concentrate more on prayer and chanting, and some focus more on inner stillness and meditation. Most of the temples I attended focused on prayer and chanting. Thus, my parents did not know how to meditate. My parents and I chanted every night before going to bed. In Buddhism, chanting is like a balm or ointment for the soul, and meditation is like the medication that purifies and heals the soul.

MY PERSONAL JOURNEY TO PEACE

I started my journey to inner peace over thirty-five years ago. I have had the opportunity to go on many meditation retreats in Thailand and have been fortunate enough to practice many different methods, such as the four foundations of mindfulness training (anapanasati, or "awareness of the breath"), walking meditation, abdominal concentration, and breathing meditation. One day, as I was studying for my bachelor's degree in economics at Kasetsart University in Bangkok, my dear friend invited me to the temple where there was a meditation class using the Dhammakāya, or Middle Way Meditation, technique. I felt very comfortable and relaxed. After learning this new technique, I had the chance to join many beautiful retreats in Thailand with the Dhammakāya Foundation. I never felt the same after each retreat. The world always looked brighter and more beautiful in many ways. Nothing had changed outside, but inside there was a growing feeling of peace and deep contentment. I learned that true happiness lies inside each one of us, and everyone can access it. I realized that people all around the world are searching for the same thing—happiness and peace—and people travel the whole world to find it. It was amazing that here it was, right inside of me, all along.

At that time, I developed a strong goal in my mind to help people find true inner peace and happiness through meditation. I wanted to share what I had found. I have always felt deep gratitude toward my friend who first invited me to meditate, because without him I would never have begun my journey to peace. I have the deepest gratitude for the abbot of the Dhammakāya meditation technique, Luang Pu Wat Paknam, and the founder of the Dhammakāya Temple, Luang Phor Dhammajayo, who work tirelessly to spread the teaching of the Middle Way to help everyone in this world discover true inner peace and happiness. I will always remember that one of the most important things along the spiritual journey is to have virtuous friends and teachers who lead you down the right path in life. I developed a strong intention in my mind to become such a friend to others, and help them along their journey to peace, no matter how big or small my role was.

STRUGGLE TO PEACE

My husband and I emigrated from Thailand to the United States in 1983. After learning how to meditate, I was able to connect to different teachers from the Dhammakāya temple in Thailand and all around the world, and I began a small meditation group with friends and family at my home. We listened to live chanting and meditation broadcasts from Thailand monthly, and have continued for over 20 years now.

I wish that everyone in the world was able to feel the happiness that I experience through meditation. My dream was to build a meditation center to teach people how to meditate and find true peace and happiness. I began searching for a place to build a meditation center that would be easily accessible for all.

In 2007, I purchased a home with two small cottages on a main street in Mobile, Alabama. We had a monk from Thailand, Venerable Wutthichai Photichai (or Venerable "Woody"), living in the house at the time to help teach meditation. A few Americans, mostly Asian Americans from the surrounding area, came to meditate with us.

We applied for nonprofit status, and were approved, then applied to the City for a permit to use our house to host regular meditation classes. Many of the surrounding neighbors came to our public hearing to oppose us, some of them citing religious and traffic concerns. We received multiple warnings from the City that all group religious activities such as meditation were prohibited. The City Council recommended denial. We withdrew our application, and for the time my dream of building a meditation center was crushed. I was left brokenhearted with an empty dream.

First location for Mediation Center of Alabama -
Cottage House in Mobile, Alabama

Two years later, a teaching monk from the Dhammakāya Temple came to visit us. He guided a meditation class and encouraged me not to give up and to continue to pursue my dream. I began to revive my dream of building a meditation center once again. Professionally, I own a shopping mall and operate a local Thai restaurant. I converted one of the rooms in our shopping center and started our first weekly meditation class in February of 2009. The class was taught by Dhammakāya monks and laypeople certified from the Dhammakāya Temple utilizing video conferencing calls. Everyone seemed very happy.

Current Meditation Center on Airport Blvd., in the heart of Mobile, Alabama

Our dear teaching monk, a Theravada Buddhist monk named Venerable Pratya Sotthiyothin, taught us the very first month. Some days there was only one student, and I will always remember what he said— "Don't worry, it only takes one person to change the world." All our teachers were shining examples that one person could have an impact on this world, and they provided me with constant inspiration. Mr. Robert Mawson, to whom this book is dedicated, was our first teacher to teach us regularly and visit our center for yearly retreats. Mr. Mawson taught us nearly every week until he passed away in 2014. He had undergone a heart transplant by the well-known Dr. Oz and was filmed for the Discovery Channel to show the difference meditation made in his recovery. He was defibrillated back to life multiple times, and one magazine called him the "Medical Miracle Man." He even taught us once from his hospital bed when he was very ill. His great love and dedication to his students, and sense of peace, was boundless. His spirit was indomitable, and his positivity and joy were effervescent. To know him was to love him. The Meditation Center of Alabama is forever grateful to Mr. Robert Mawson, our dear teacher.

We began our center with a Thursday meditation class. The first few years, I spent a great deal of time with very few volunteers to help run our nonprofit organization. Drs. Cay and Kent Welsh, co-writers of this book, and the late Craig Lindsey were the main volunteers who helped to run our center for many years. My daughter, Nena, helped with social media and emails while she was in medical school.

One of our meditation students, Estela Dorn, helped to have an article written about our center in the local newspaper. After news began to spread, attendance began to increase, and we added two more classes to our weekly schedule—a Monday night silent meditation class led by Drs. Cay and Kent Welsh, and a Wednesday night class for beginners. After class on

Wednesdays and Thursdays, all students enjoyed a vegetarian meal prepared by my Thai restaurant. We held weekend retreats with visiting instructors two to three times a year.

Our meditation classes have been conducted at the second location in my shopping mall for over ten years now, and we open our doors to people from all backgrounds, religions, and walks of life without any fee or charge, donations accepted. We teach everyone who comes to our center the Dhammakāya or Middle Way meditation method, a simple and easy meditation technique based on relaxation of the body and mind. Most are beginners, who are surprised to find that 45 minutes of guided meditation with loving kindness passes by relatively quickly.

After being in a commercial setting for some time, I began to dream of building a meditation retreat center for the community in a quiet, secluded area. Though I was deeply grateful to have been able to start the Meditation Center at all, I quickly realized the hustle and bustle of sirens, ambulances, and passerby was becoming an obstacle for many beginners who came to our center. I began to look for a secluded property to build a retreat center. I went through many options, and finally came upon a beautiful seven-acre piece of land on Dog River. I learned from my previous experiences that it was important to get planning approval from the city. I took all the recommended steps to ensure this property would not face the same obstacles I had encountered before. A pre-planning Commissioner's meeting was held, and no concerns were voiced from the City. I was given an application to get planning approval. And finally, my husband, Dr. Prasit Nimityongskul (Pediatric Orthopedist), and I purchased the property. Little did we know that the biggest obstacles were yet to come.

Our greatest challenge was the next-door neighbor, who set up a well-organized opposition from the surrounding area citing environmental, noise, and traffic concerns to the Planning Commissioners at two public hearings. We modified our plans, complied with all city requirements, and remained willing to make all necessary changes. We were not being treated as a nonprofit religious group, and our religious nature remained unacknowledged even after providing evidence of our Buddhist nature. The city did a traffic count on my street and confirmed that there were no traffic issues relating to building the Meditation Retreat Center on our subject property. There were no churches asked to prove their religious status, but we were asked to provide proof of our Buddhist nature.

We were treated, not as a religious organization, but rather as a commercial organization and denied zoning permissions.

House on Dog River – Proposed site for MCA
Retreat Center

The obstacles in my life have served to make me stronger, more resilient, and test my resolve of spreading inner peace. I had to dig deep to find my purpose and stay true to my dream over the past two decades. I have been tested repeatedly. I realize that it would have been easier to give up. But then I would lose out on the opportunity to bring peace to many people who are still searching for it. And from my heart, I would like to help them no matter the obstacle. Because of these obstacles, I feel the community needs peace even more. There is no happiness without sadness, no praise without blame, no gain without loss —these are the Buddha's teachings. It is our struggles that make our accomplishments meaningful and rewarding, and we are lucky enough to have this life to make a difference for others. We should all try our best, regardless of naysayers, to make a difference. I will continue to strive to build peace for the community. As Luang Phor Dhammajayo teaches us (Abbot of the Dhammakāya Temple), "For the mind that refuses to give up, there is no obstacle too great in this world."

A Beautiful Sangha

One of the greatest benefits of coming together to meditate is the benefit of practicing in a supportive environment. A sangha is a group of like-minded people that encourages each other along the path to goodness. Meditation is not something that most people do naturally until they begin to see the long-term benefits that only come from a consistent practice. Thus, having a sangha, or group of like-minded people, to support you is an essential source of encouragement. The experience of meditation is different from learning its theories. It is like eating a dish from a foreign country. You can describe to a foreigner what spaghetti tastes like in a thousand words, but this person will never truly understand until they eat it for themselves. Ultimately, nobody can find peace for you. No one can take medication for you as much as they want you to heal. The only person who can do it is you. Having a wise teacher and virtuous friends makes the path to inner peace easier, filled with joy and constant encouragement in times of difficulty. Without the support of the Meditation Center of Alabama Sangha, I am not sure if I could have persevered for so many years to build a meditation center and work towards a retreat center. To this day, some of the kindest, most generous, and amazing people I have ever met have come into my life by walking through the front doors of our meditation center or volunteered to teach our Sangha.

SPREADING PEACE

After hosting tri-weekly classes for some time, we began to grow outward in the hopes of spreading peace to a greater part of the community. My daughter, Nena, started the first ever Meditation and Mindfulness Club at the University of South Alabama. The club routinely invites clinical psychologists and long-time members and volunteers Drs. Cay Kent Welsh to teach evidence-based lectures on self-development and personal growth. The USA Meditation and Mindfulness club, advised by Leo Denton, has introduced meditation and wellness to thousands of students who have learned how to better cope with the stressors of college life. Yoga studios such as Kudzu Aerial (founder Megrez Mosher) and Above and Beyond Yoga studio (founders Shoshana and Jake Treichel) have invited us to teach regular classes at their studios; most recently, we have joined hands with Central Presbyterian Church, headed by pastor Chris Bullock. Long-time member and volunteer Leo Denton, a lifelong Christian with a goal to spread world peace through inner peace, has spearheaded this project to help make mindfulness and spirituality available to all. Our dear teaching monk, Phra Nicholas Thanissaro, has come to visit us every year for the past four years for a series of lectures and a weekend meditation retreat at the Grand Hotel in the nearby city of Point Clear, Alabama. We will continue to host public lectures and retreats to benefit the community.

If you were to ask me, "Why fight so hard for this? Why endure what you have been through where the opposition to your message is so overwhelming at times?"

My answer would be simple. Because I believe in the message, I carry.

I believe our world is made up of people searching for healing in one form or another. If you can help a person find healing, you can change the world. Sometimes you must fight for the right to help others. The center, my journey, and this book are evidence of my belief in my message.

Within the chapters to come, you will read about the power of healing found through meditation. You will read methods, techniques, and personal stories of those who have experienced healing changes because they saw the power of meditation in their daily lives. This is not just a "How-to" book. This is an opportunity for you to learn what has directed my life. I invite you to continue through the learning process as you read and, in this choice to continue, discover the healing power of meditation in your life as well.

2

WHAT IS MEDITATION?

SERENA NIMITYONGSKUL M.D.

My Journey to Peace

During my first two-week meditation retreat on a beautiful mountain resort in Thailand, my life forever changed. Prior to attending, I had recently dropped out of college and lost direction in life. I was not sure what I wanted to do or why. During this life-changing meditation retreat, I was led by teaching monks and lay staff to cultivate moment-to-moment mindfulness, awareness of the present moment, and gratefulness for every moment of my life. We started the day with meditation and chanting, mindful eating and listening to wisdom talks on the purpose of life, creating and developing good habits and fulfilling our life's potential—which I discovered started from finding peace and clarity within to know yourself and what you really want in life. I began to develop a new appreciation for life and my purpose in the world. I wanted to do something useful with my life. I came back with a burning desire to help others and share peace and light to the world. I re-gained clarity and direction and began once again to strive to become a medical doctor. I felt at that time in my life the best way to help the world was to become a doctor. As I went through residency, many specialties captured my interest. I saw people being given a second chance at life. I noticed that some people who had their limbs amputated or were dealing with life threatening illnesses seemed to have a resilience and positivity that I did not. It was incredibly inspiring to feel the strength of the human spirit. During my psychiatry rotation, I met others who had everything you could ever want in life—a beautiful family, wonderful career, and wealth; but they wanted to end their life and did not seem to have anything to live for. This paradox made me think again about the source of happiness and suffering in life. Was it truly external, or was there a source and wellspring of happiness that could be cultivated inside regardless of external circumstances?

Thus, I began my lifelong search within to understand my own mind through the practice of meditation, to help unlock the key to happiness for myself and all those around me. I am still on this journey. I was given the greatest opportunity in life by my mother, to volunteer and help build the Meditation Center of Alabama. Helping others at their darkest moments in life has taught me the importance of self-love and self-care, mindfulness and inner peace that can be found at the center of every storm. No matter how stormy it may seem, there is a refuge of peace, a stillness that exists at the center. And if you can stay there long enough, the storm will surely pass, and the sun will shine again.

Through my volunteer work, I was given the incredible opportunity to train to become a Middle Way Meditation Coach through The Middle Way Meditation Institute and became a Certified Meditation and Mindfulness Trainer through World Peace Initiative. I felt incredibly lucky to have been given this opportunity to learn from knowledgeable teaching monks and be inspired by individuals from all around the world who were actively spreading the knowledge of mindfulness and inner peace. I came back and began to work on my social anxiety and painfully shy personality little by little. I went from not being able to speak in front of people to teaching meditation to a roomful of doctors at the Alabama Physician's Psychiatric Association.

I have witnessed first-hand how people's lives can transform through the practice of meditation. Some people come to the meditation center after a divorce, after being given a terminal diagnosis, or other crisis in their life. Some have come struggling with addictions and have been able to stay sober and remain clean while developing a healthier lifestyle. Some are now even meditation teachers. When you have the right attitude and strength of mind, there is no obstacle that is too difficult to overcome and no mountain too high to climb. By staying in the present moment, you learn to enjoy every step, and that makes every journey more worthwhile and meaningful.

For me, the greatest happiness of being a meditation instructor is right after leading a guided meditation. When I open my eyes, I see a roomful of people who are brighter, lighter, and happier than before. Their smiles light up my world and make everything worth it. One time I taught a 30-minute meditation to a roomful of patients in a group home setting. These patients have chronic and debilitating mental illnesses such as a primary psychotic disorder or borderline personality disorder and must live with some assistance and oversight to remain safe and stable. I did not have any real expectations in teaching them. One of them I had even admitted to the hospital before when she was acutely psychotic. I led them through a guided visualization of being at the beach, relaxing every part of their bodies while breathing in deeply and slowly and allowing their thoughts to pass by like watching clouds. At the end, I led a guided loving kindness meditation for self-love and sharing peace and positivity to all fellow beings in the world. Afterwards, every single one of them looked brighter and like a weight had been lifted off their shoulders. One man who had chronic schizophrenia said "Wow! I feel like I just want to go out and help people in this world." His statement touched me deeply. The lady who I had previously admitted to the hospital looked brighter, happier, and said she felt light like a weight had been lifted off her shoulders and asked if she could do this every day. It was one of the happiest moments for me, to see those struggling with debilitating and life-long mental illness benefit from meditation. I knew after that class that if they could do it, anyone could. All it takes is a willingness to learn and practice.

3

THE CONCEPTS OF MEDITATION & LOVING KINDNESS

SERENA NIMITYONGSKUL M.D.

A Mindful Driver

Imagine this: you are a bus driver driving to your favorite destination. Along the way, there are passengers that come and go. Some are more pleasant, some smile kindly, some have negative or critical words to say, and some are just downright rude. As the bus driver, you have the choice to stop your bus and choose who you would like to interact with. The passengers are the thoughts in your mind. The ideas and commentary are the story lines that go on in your mind throughout the day. Some passengers will be helpful and may even help you drive the bus. Some may cause you to get into a wreck if you let them take over. It is our job as a responsible driver to be mindful of the road, where we are going, and what is happening inside and outside of our bus. Because accidents can be caused both by us and the cars around us.

A wonderful tool that will teach you how your bus operates, how to stay safe on the roads, how to allow the passengers on your bus to come and go without getting into a fight, and how to let off each negative person, is mindfulness. Mindfulness allows us to be in the present moment and be aware, allowing our thoughts to be like clouds passing through the sky. We begin to see that thoughts are not true or false, but rather harmful or helpful. We can choose to let them be or let them go, without having to interact or engage, and continue our journey with more self-acceptance and peace.

A Universal Tool

Meditation is a tool that will train your mind to be more calm, more peaceful, and more still. Everyone has access to this tool. Meditation has nothing to do with religion or culture, although it is embedded within some religious traditions. But the practice and results of meditation do not depend upon the acceptance of any religious beliefs. When your mind has more clarity and less mental chatter you can make better decisions for yourself and the people around you. As you make better decisions, you become more effective in whatever job or goal you are pursuing.

Numerous celebrities and public figures have espoused the benefits of meditation in their daily lives. Entrepreneur Russell Simmons (co-founder of Def Jam records) says, "You want to be awake during the day. I do not want the noise to separate me from whatever greatness is in here. You want to be able to get what you imagine. You want to be able to operate from that awakened state. Meditation gives you that."

Oprah Winfrey brought meditation into her workplace. "I brought TM [transcendental meditation] into Harpo studios to teach me and my team how to meditate. Seven led to 70, 70 led to 270, now everybody in the company meditates at nine o'clock in the morning, 4:30 in the afternoon. No matter what is going on, we stop we meditate. This way of being still with ourselves, coming back to a center, and recognizing something is more important than you, more important than the work you are doing, brings a kind of energy and intensity, an intensity that we have never had before. You cannot imagine what has happened in the company! People who used to have migraines do not. People are sleeping better and having better relationships. People interact better with others. It has been fantastic! The one thing I want to continue to do, is center myself every day. I want to make that a daily practice for myself, because I am 1000% better when I do, when I take myself back to something bigger than myself ..."

Actor Jim Carrey also agrees. He said, "I think on a widespread level it's being picked up by everybody now. It is being understood as something more than religious nutty thing. It is a system of teaching yourself how to get into a state of relaxation that affects your entire life and the quality of your life. I do it. I've done it for a while, and I recommend it highly."

These celebrities are from different backgrounds and fields and illustrate that no matter what your goal is, what your passion is in life, or what you believe in, we all have a superpower that we can cultivate to accomplishing our goals. Clarity of mind will help you to be a better mother, sister, brother, Christian, Hindu, or Muslim. Meditation is the language of peace, and peace is universal. Though we all look different on the outside, when we close our eyes and access the stillness inside, we begin to understand that we speak a common language—the language of peace and loving kindness. This powerful language transcends all boundaries and cultures and can positively change the world for the better.

SELF-DISCOVERY AND INNER WISDOM

Becoming more self-aware and mindful offers us a freedom to not always be fused with the endless stream of thoughts and mental chatter. A strength and clarity of mind arises with regular practice, and eventually one becomes more aware of what really matters in life. It is like taking the rose-colored glasses off. You see yourself as you really are. Meditation is like cleaning the dust off a mirror. And sometimes the things we see are not always positive. And that is ok. We are human, and we all have the capability to make good or bad decisions. Mindfulness gives us the space to teach and train ourselves to respond more skillfully and gracefully to the problems around and within us.

When we sit in stillness, we go beyond the superficial and dive deep into the soul; we become one with who we are on the deepest level. We make peace with ourselves and accept ourselves without judgment. When the mind is bright and clear, a feeling of loving kindness, wanting others to be happy and peaceful, naturally arises. Happy people tend to make other people happy. Unhappy people tend to make other people unhappy.

Everyone suffers in some way, regardless of wealth, status, or station in life; all are affected by the same conditions of loss and gain, sadness and happiness, praise, and blame. Learning how to deal with these more skillfully is a choice and a practice. Thich Naht Hanh says, "if you know how to suffer, you suffer less." Through meditation, a greater sense of acceptance for ourselves and others is achieved as we begin to understand the true nature of reality. Can you imagine a world filled with people who are at peace with themselves and others? It would be a very beautiful place indeed!

PLEASURE VS HAPPINESS

The happiness from meditation is different from the happiness gained in the outside world. Happiness from the outside world is what we normally think of as pleasure. Pleasure comes when you get the newest iPhone. But when the next iPhone model comes out and you want that one, you suffer. Then, when you get the newest model, the cycle perpetuates. Craving and attachment have the downside of leaving you wanting more. This leaves us unsatisfied with our current state, taking us away from the present moment. Psychologists say we spend 45% of our thoughts in the past and 45% of our thoughts in the future. The amount of time we spend in the present moment is actually very small. Happiness from meditation is a happiness from non-attachment, a feeling of wellbeing that arises from peace and contentment in the present moment. This happiness is sustainable and exists despite changing external circumstances. The Greeks had two words for happiness: hedonia and eudaimonia. Hedonia is what we take from the world to be happy. Eudaimonia is what we give to the world to give us happiness. Happiness derived from cultivating goodness is a self-sustaining, internal state of mind.

We live most of our lives in a whirlwind of thoughts and analysis. Sometimes the thoughts and distractions get the better of us, causing the most beautiful things in our life to pass by unnoticed. Such is the situation when we see a couple having dinner together, both busy playing on their cell phones. They miss the human connection and the happiness from just being with each other. Technology is inadvertently engineering the next generation to be less present and less mindful. But there is something we can do about it. It is not too late. Learning mindfulness skills, such as coming back to the breath, can prevent us from being victims of distraction, and help us take back control over our lives and move in a more positive direction.

THE MIND

Human beings are made of a body and a mind. A mind without a body is a spirit. A body without a mind is a corpse. The mind is like the software and the brain is the hardware on which the software runs. Training the mind is like upgrading the software. Even if you have the latest HP model, if you are using Windows 7 it will not be very efficient. You can upgrade your software to Windows 10 and the computer will run much more effectively. No matter what meditation method you practice, there are two key elements: relaxation and mindfulness (or calm and consciousness). No matter what method you practice, these are the two key ingredients. Nearly all meditation methods are helpful. The most important thing is that you utilize them to create some benefit in your life.

Mindfulness is a state of mind where we are non-reactively and non-judgmentally in the present moment. Whatever is going on in our minds, whether we have thoughts or no thoughts, feelings, or no feelings, we accept it in stillness. This stillness does not necessarily mean a mind without thoughts, though it can be. Many people think they cannot meditate because they have too many thoughts. Thinking is part of the human experience. It is natural, to be expected, and a wonderful thing to be able to think and analyze. It is because we have thoughts that we can meditate and train our minds.

You can imagine the mind is like a glass of water. When you are born, the water is clear and bright. If you put a rose behind this glass you could easily see the beauty of the rose and you could feel the happiness around, you. When you were young, happiness was simple. When children eat ice cream, they smile; when they lose it, they cry. When mother brings a new toy, the child stops crying and smiles again. Happiness is very instant.

Once we are older, we go to school, compete in work, start a family or a business, we start to add many colors into the water. Red for anger, blue for depression, green when someone makes us feel upset. The same glass, but now our experience is different. When you look through it at the rose, beauty is still there, but something inside is not clear and blocks you from feeling happiness. This is the world we are experiencing. There is external good, but spiritually we are not clean and clear to experience happiness.

There are many people who are rich and successful but do not feel happy inside. They get angry easily and they feel negativity easily because the glass is not clear inside them. When we meditate, we do a very simple practice—we put the glass down. We let everything sink down to the bottom. Simple, right? Simply relax and let everything sink down to the bottom. Life becomes complicated, so we need to go back to simplicity. Sit, relax, do nothing, and let everything settle down to the bottom. That is the easiest way to describe meditation.

OBSERVING YOUR THOUGHTS

In meditation, we sit and rest our minds. Imagine that you are lying down relaxing on a beautiful beach, taking a vacation for yourself, watching the turquoise blue waters dancing in front of you and the spacious blue skies spreading out all around you. This is the attitude we have when we come to meditate—take a break and relax. As we relax, however, we notice thoughts in our mind. We can treat our thoughts as if they are birds passing through the sky. When you are relaxed on the beach and a bird flies over your head, you know it flew over your head, but you do not care; you let it go and continue to enjoy the wind from the beach and the sound of the ocean. You already have this skill. We are not teaching you anything new here. You have achieved this state of mind before. You use this same skill in meditation.

During meditation, when a thought comes flying through your mind like a bird, you let the bird fly. You do not stop and try to talk to the bird! There is a saying: "You can't stop a bird from flying over your head, but you can stop the bird from making a nest on your head." What does this mean? When a bird flies over your head and you are relaxed on the beach, you do not care, you are able to let it go. But if a bird flies over your head and you begin to think "What kind of bird is it? Where is it going? Is it a boy or a girl?", now you've created a nest on your head. We do this all the time!

We are constantly stuck in certain thought loops and ruminations, playing similar story lines over and over each day. Do not get me wrong, being able to analyze is a good thing, and we need to be able to think clearly and make good decisions for ourselves. But it is when we cannot stop thinking that we develop problems such as insomnia and anxiety due to constant worries and stress. And this excessive worry causes our sympathetic nervous system to run awry.

The sympathetic nervous system is the "fight or flight" system of our body. It is responsible for activating us in times of danger by increasing our heart rate, pumping more blood to the body, and increasing blood to our organs. The development of the "fight or flight" system is evolutionarily advantageous. We need to be able to quickly assess the environment for dangers. Back in the days when we were hunters and gatherers, if there was a saber tooth tiger after us, we needed to be able to run away quickly. This is a very important system.

Nowadays, it is less likely for a tiger to be threatening our lives. However, chronic stress such as work, school, and family are causing our "fight or flight" systems to run in overdrive, leading to health complications such as high blood pressure, migraines, and even life-threatening health problems such as strokes. Sixty percent of doctor visits in the United States are due to chronic stress.3 Meditation, in contrast, turns on the parasympathetic nervous system, the "rest or digest" system, to invoke the relaxation response and tone down our harried sympathetic nervous system response.

GETTING THE EFFORT RIGHT

We cannot force our mind to be still. This is an important concept. Imagine a crying baby. You cannot make a baby stop crying by forcing it to be quiet. It will only cry louder. If you pat the baby on its back or rock it back and forth, giving it a nice and loving environment, it will eventually stop crying on its own. The mind is the same. When we come to meditate, we are very kind and gentle to our minds. Just like you cannot force yourself to fall asleep, you cannot force the mind to quiet down. But as we relax and be kind and gentle to ourselves, the mind will quiet down on its own.

The mind is like a monkey. When you sit down to meditate, you will notice your thoughts are constantly jumping around, like a monkey swinging from branch to branch. Sometimes we do not even finish one thought and we are off to the next one. This state of constant distractibility leads to forgetfulness, and even attention deficit disorder in some cases. So how do we make a monkey sit still? Give it a banana, or something to focus on. Then the monkey will sit still. Our minds are not that much different.

The mind has a unique characteristic of being able to think of only one thing at a time. When people multitask, they are simply switching from one thought to the next very rapidly. Some people are very good at multitasking, but it does divide your attention. Because of this characteristic, however, we know if we think of something, or someone, our mind is with that object or person. For example, right now, take a moment and imagine the sun....

There is no sun in the room, right? You are using your mind, and you know your mind is with the sun. In this same way, we can use different objects in meditation to capture our mind and train it to be in the present moment. When we train our minds in this way, we develop an inner light or brightness. When the sun shines its brightness and warmth is felt by everyone it touches. In the same way, your inner peace will be felt by your family, friends, and the community. A better you create a more peaceful world. Sustainable world peace is possible through the attainment of each person's own individual peace.

MINDFULNESS TOOLS

There are several meditation methods that we can use to capture the mind. The essence of meditation is maintaining consciousness and calm throughout your session. However, the mind tends to wander; methods are used to help "tame our monkey" and calm the mind down. Different people have different personalities, thus different methods are used by different people according to the nature of their mind. If it makes you feel more peaceful and more relaxed, that method matches with the nature of your mind. All methods lead to the same point—observation with a still and neutral mind. Just like a boat is used to cross a river, you can choose whatever boat you like to cross over from stress to relaxation. Once you have reached the other side, there is no need to carry the boat with you. Drop it and continue to maintain consciousness and calm and observe whatever happens.

An easy method is to follow the breath. The breath is something natural, something with a natural rhythm that is easy to follow. You can breathe deeply now. Slowly, deeply, and gently, three times. Notice the turning point of your breath in the center of your stomach. This point is the home base of your mind, the center of your body. Imagine that you wanted to balance a round object on your finger. If you placed your finger on the side of the object it would fall, but if you placed the object at the center of gravity in the middle it would be still and balanced. The same with our bodies. The body's anatomical center of gravity is at the turning point of the breath.

For those who can easily feel the center, you may rest your mind at the turning point of the breath or have a general feeling of being centered. Imagine you are sitting alone in a wide-open field, and your mind has expanded throughout the entire universe, and you are the center. Rest your mind softly and gently wherever it is most comfortable. After maintaining consciousness and calm for some time, the mind will naturally become more still and centered and come to rest at the most balanced point on its own. When you drop a napkin, the law of gravity automatically brings the napkin to rest on the ground. When we relax the body and mind, the center will magnetize the mind to fall in the most balanced state on its own. You do not have to do anything at all, just rest your mind in the most comfortable position and maintain consciousness and calm. Imagine a pendulum being pulled by different forces. If you let go (relaxation), it will automatically come to rest in stillness at the center.

If you find it easy to imagine and are more creatively inclined, you may use visualization. The mind is a feeling. It is not like trying to see something as vivid or clear as our eyes or an HD camera. Imagine you are walking outside on a beautiful sunny day. You feel the sun warm and bright on your face. You bring that feeling inside your stomach like an anchor for the mind. You can use any object to keep your mind at the most comfortable spot. The feeling of a bright and peaceful moon, a bright star, a clear and light soap bubble, or even a cross—whatever is easiest for you to visualize. The simpler the object the easier.

You may also use a mantra if that is easier for you. If you love to listen to music or have a barrage of thoughts in your mind, you may enjoy this method. A mantra is simply a word phrase to capture all the thoughts into one, and later, the one can become nothing. An easy phrase is "clear and bright," or "relaxed and comfortable." You can use any word phrase you like, such as "peace in, peace out," or "breathing in, breathing out, I feel completely at peace." The goal is to choose something peaceful that matches with the nature of your mind, not something too complicated that may stir up more thoughts in the mind. When using the mantra, do it playfully. Imagine there is an iPod in the center of your stomach. You simply press play. The mantra repeats at a speed that is most comfortable for you. The mantra is repeated silently in your mind like a song that captures your thoughts. Simply choose a method and observe. If your mind wanders, do a "bicep curl" for the mind. We are rarely mindful enough to realize the moment that our minds begin to wander. So, the act of just noticing that your mind has wandered and gently bringing it back to the breath, or center of the body, is a wonderful feat. This is a "bicep curl" for the mind, strengthening that muscle of awareness to remain in the present moment.

The Indicator

Whatever method you choose, the indicator that you are on the right path is a relaxed and comfortable feeling, even if you are doing nothing and just observing. If you use a method that makes you more and more tense, that method does not match with the nature of your mind on that day. Keep in mind that on different days you may utilize different methods. Some days when you have so much monkey mind, the mantra helps to cut down on those thoughts. Some days you feel relaxed enough to just observe and do nothing. Follow your feeling—the most relaxed and comfortable path for you that day is the right one.

4

HOW TO MEDITATE

SERENA NIMITYONGSKUL M.D.

STEPS TO MEDITATION

The steps to meditation are very simple. When you are first starting off your practice it may be helpful to follow the steps or a guided meditation (resources at the end of this chapter). However, as you begin to practice more and more you will find what works best for you, finding flexibility and individuality within the technique. It is like learning how to cook. First you follow the recipe and after some time you will begin to prepare things in your own way, making adjustments to fit your own unique style. The key to success is the consistency of practice.

1. RELAX THE BODY

Get comfy: Begin by finding a comfortable, quiet place for yourself, maybe at a time early in the morning before the kids have woken up or late in the evening when things have died down. Begin with gentle stretching on a chair or on the floor, whatever feels most comfortable for you. A nice upright position will help you to maintain a relaxed but alert state. Having your hands palms upwards will help open your chest so you can breathe more easily. You can place your hands palms upwards on your knees or in the center of your lap. Throughout your practice you are welcome to adjust your position mindfully and gently.

Soft gaze: You might like to start with your eyes open but relaxed. Or you can allow your eyes to soften and gently close almost as if you are about to fall asleep. Closing your eyes with an almost feather light touch. Being careful not to squeeze them shut.

Relaxing the body: We can begin our practice with a body scan to relax every part of our body from the top of our heads down to the tips of our toes. Like a refreshing shower or stream of water that washes over you, relaxing the muscles around your eyes, allowing your shoulders to drop naturally, relaxing your torso and legs, washing away all the tension and stress from your body.

2. RELAX THE MIND

We then turn our attention to relaxing the mind. Like a traveler walking down a long airport carrying two heavy bags, the past and the future. Finally, he decides to put the baggage down, sit down and take a rest. He feels much lighter and free from all burdens in the mind. In the same way we relax our minds by putting aside our to-do lists, responsibilities, and stressors about family, work, school or friends. Just putting everything aside for these precious moments to come back and enjoy the present.

Contentment and ease: You might like to imagine that you are sitting in your favorite place in nature. A wide-open mountain top, the beautiful spacious skies or an open spacious beach with turquoise blue waters sparkling in front of you. As you take a seat you release all the cares and worries from your mind. Breathing in the refreshing and pure air all around you. Letting go of all the negativities from your mind. Maybe the sun is gently shining today, perfectly at ease in both body and mind. Allowing your mind to be vast and spacious, like the clear blue skies.

Everything is just right as it is. Nothing to do, nothing to achieve. Just breathing and being.

3. MAINTAIN CONSCIOUSNESS AND CALM

Continue to maintain the balance between relaxation and mindfulness, or consciousness and calm, at the most comfortable spot. Maybe inside your body somewhere in the center of your stomach or wherever it feels most comfortable. Maybe you are as big as the universe and you are already in the center. The center or 'home' of the mind is wherever you feel most comfortable. From there simply observe whatever happens. Not being the actor or director but simply an observer, allowing the inner experience to unfold naturally.

4. ALLOW THE MIND TO STILL (DO NOTHING)

As you continue to observe with patience, neutrality and acceptance of the present moment maintain this balance between relaxation and mindfulness, the golden path. Your feeling is your indicator. If you are more tense, you have begun to think and react again. Simply come back to the breath, to your mindfulness object (warm sun, peaceful moon, etc) or a mantra to capture the thoughts in the mind. When you feel relaxed and comfortable again you can let the tool go and go back to being in the observer's seat, mindfully and gently aware of whatever happens without judgement. The ultimate goal is to do nothing, sit back, and allow the mind to still on its own. However, we tend to think and do. And when we cannot sit back and do nothing the mindfulness tools are there to help you to navigate the waters to reach the shore of stillness and tranquility.

TROUBLESHOOTING YOUR INNER EXPERIENCE

Mindfulness tools & the indicator: As discussed in the previous chapter everyone has a different personality. Different mindfulness tools will help different people relax. Try different ones to find the one that works best for you. The feeling of being centered or resting your mind at the most comfortable spot, visualizing a neutral object (remember visualization is a feeling. You do not want to see the sun with your eyes but simply feel the warmth of the sun, that is using the mind) and a mantra or short word phrase to capture all the thoughts into one. The indicator that you are on the right path is a sabai (pronounced 'sa-bye,' Thai word meaning relaxed in both body and mind) and comfortable feeling that grows as you use the tool. Even if you are doing nothing at all but feeling sabai, that is a sign that you are 100% on the right path. No need to do anything at all if it feels sabai for you. Just observe your reactions, your thoughts, and your feelings. Everything is impermanent and will come and go if we can sit back and let it be.

Neutrality and non-striving: It is important to approach our practice with a beginners mind. Like this is the first time you have ever meditated in your life, completely detached from all previous experiences. No matter how good the moment was or may have seemed, if we let the past go, we make space for something new and more peaceful to flow in. Neutrality and acceptance is key. All thoughts, feelings and emotions are completely normal. Simply observe and allow them to come and go. For those who have extensive experience meditating sometimes refined expectations begin to appear in the mind after years of practice. If you find you are striving to reach or attain some goal in meditation, simply adjust your attitude. You are not sitting down to achieve anything at all. Simply sitting to chill out, take a break and give your mind a rest.

Tension, reset if needed: If you are feeling more tense it is a sign that you may be thinking or trying too hard. This is a normal occurrence, just observe and let it be. If you are not able to observe or do nothing, simply come back to your breath or the mindfulness tool that is most comfortable for you. If these don't work and you begin to struggle more simply reset. Never be afraid to reset. Open your eyes, relax, take some deep breaths, do some stretching or take a walk. Whenever you're ready, gently return back to your mat until you feel like closing your eyes again.

If you find tension to be a regular occurrence, make it a habit to take your time prior to starting your practice. Take as much time as you need to stretch, relax, de-stress and cultivate patience. Do not rush to close your eyes. Simply soften your gaze and sit relaxingly until your body and mind are completely at ease, allowing your eyes to close on their own.

Sleepy mind: Sometimes we may feel too relaxed and get sleepy. This is also a normal occurrence. Sometimes you are tired and need to rest. However, you may refresh yourself by breathing in deeply and straightening your back, opening your eyes, or even visualizing a brighter object such as a bright star or a very bright sun. You might even keep a cold cloth next to you to wipe your face and refresh yourself during meditation. Outside of the round make note of how much rest you are getting, if you are drinking enough water, and if you are feeling refreshed enough prior to the start of meditation. If you are very sleepy you might need a quick power nap prior to starting your practice, or choose a time of day when you are more relaxed and alert (early morning or evening).

Being mindful throughout the day: The outside round directly affects the inside round. Thus, continue to maintain the balance between relaxation and mindfulness throughout your daily activities. Start small and build up. Choose one activity like folding clothes, brushing your teeth, or washing the dishes to practice being mindful and relaxed. You might notice your breath, or feel centered like your mind is as big and spacious as the whole world and you are working or doing your chores in the center, or maybe you feel a bright sun or calming moon at your center. Do what feels most natural and relaxed for you.

Some people set an alarm to remind themselves to take a mindfulness break every hour. This can be as simple as 5 deep breaths while walking down the hallway. Or if you have a minute to sit down relax your shoulders, soften your gaze, breathe deeply, and allow your mind to settle down. Giving yourself mini mindfulness breaks, similar to a coffee break, can help you feel refreshed and relaxed throughout the day. You may find yourself moving through challenges with more ease and grace.

A good time to practice meditation is upon waking up and before going to bed. When you wake up don't jump up and check your phone right away. Take a moment to breathe in, feel how lucky you are to be alive another day (so many people did not wake up today) and close your eyes, allowing your mind to center and still for a few minutes. And when you feel peaceful maybe spreading loving kindness and making positive affirmations for the day. At night prior to sleeping is another excellent time to meditate and spread loving kindness. It helps you to release the burdens of the day, put down the to-do lists and "close the apps" on the phone or "software" of your mind. So you can power off your phone and rest peacefully.

Doubt: Some people doubt themselves as they begin their practice. This is normal human nature. Doubt is just another thought. Just observe the thought and let it go, like a bird that flies overhead. Everything in this world has a beginning, a middle and an end. Just observe the change and impermanence. Science has proven (as you will learn more in the upcoming chapters) that meditation is an evidence-based practice proven to increase mental and physical well-being. Even one deep breath or a moment of mindfulness can add a drop of peace or positivity into the ocean of your mind to color your day with more joy. Believe in the practice and ask questions to experienced instructors or fellow practitioners. You will learn as you continue the journey that most people have the same types of obstacles as we all have a mind that operates in a similar fashion. Thus, if you are unsure please join a class and ask.

Sangha and virtuous friends: As you can see there are many different types of experiences during meditation and it is always good to have the guidance of an experienced instructor or the support of a sangha, a group of like-minded people. The Buddha was once asked by his disciple Ananda about friendship. Ananda knew that having good and encouraging friends was very important for the path. He even wondered whether having good friends is half the path. "No, Ananda," the Buddha said, "having good friends isn't half of the Holy Life. Having good friends is the whole of the Holy Life." Thus, we encourage you to join the Meditation Center of Alabama's online sangha or any group nearby your home. This will help you to stay inspired, consistent and dedicated to the practice.

Consistency is the key to success: Keep in mind that meditation and cultivating positive and healthy habits takes practice. It is like learning to ride a bike. At first you fall off. Just get back up and keep going. You will get better and better with practice. It is sometimes likened to growing a tree. Imagine you want to grow an apple tree. If you put an apple seed in the ground, you will not get apples overnight. You must continue to water your tree every day with consistency of effort; one day you will be able to experience many beautiful fruits in your life.

FOUR DIVINE QUALITIES OF LOVE

The Eastern wisdom traditions give a helpful teaching on the four qualities of love. It is said that true love has these four qualities of heart, sometimes referred to as the brahma viharas (brahma meaning divine, vihara meaning home) or dwelling places of the mind. They are meant to be cultivated towards all beings unconditionally and are powerful mindfulness practices and antidotes to negativity in the mind. Practiced regularly they bring about a soft, open hearted yet wise and equanimous mind, and are a great source of joy for the practitioner.

Loving kindness: Loving kindness is a wish for everyone in this world to be happy, starting from ourselves and including all sentient beings. Loving kindness is likened to the way a mother loves her child unconditionally. With practice we can learn to extend this warm heartedness and good will towards all, starting from ourselves and rippling outwards to the ones closest to us, throughout the community to strangers, and even those who may have caused us some anger or irritation. No matter the negative consequences of one's actions loving kindness understands that at the end of the day we are all subject to the same worldly conditions and each human being is deserving of love and affection.

In the Buddha's time there was a wild elephant named Nalagiri. One day this elephant came charging towards the Buddha as he was walking. The Buddha simply put his hand out in front of him. Due to the Buddha's immense loving kindness and compassion the elephant immediately stopped in his tracks and bowed down before the Buddha. This story illustrates the transformative power that loving kindness has to change negativity and anger into peace, understanding and respect.

Many choose to end their meditation practice with a loving kindness meditation. Feel the peace, purity and brightness at the center of your being and spread it outwards like the bright sun that radiates in all directions expanding endlessly throughout the region and land, out to touch family, friends, loved ones, and ultimately rippling out to heal and purify this whole world. May all beings and animals be happy and free from suffering. May all beings be able to find true peace, and may world peace become a reality in our lifetime. Our pure wishes and feelings of goodwill help to calm our own mind, reducing negativity and irritation, and helps to calm down the people and world around us with our peace energy. Energy speaks louder than words.

A first and most important element of loving kindness is self-love. True love and compassion begins with yourself. You cannot give what you do not have. When the airplane gets bumpy and the air masks drop, they say to put the mask on yourself first, then reach over to help a friend. Thus in a difficult situation or circumstance breathe deeply, calm your own mind first then take right action having regained clarity. Take steps to love yourself unconditionally and fill your life with self-care. A healthy diet, regular exercise, positive thinking, and gratitude. All of these are the basics of good mental health. Make time everyday just for you. The most difficult circumstances require the most self-compassion (love towards yourself). You might like to try a practice of self-love. I invite you to place your hands on your heart for a moment and breathe in deeply. Feeling the rise and fall of your chest. Take a moment to send yourself pure, unconditional love and tell yourself that you love yourself very much, forgiving yourself of everything. Forgive, forget and let go. You are enough, more than enough and nobody is more deserving of your love and affection than you. You might choose to try this practice every day and see how your relationship with yourself begins to grow and blossom. Self-acceptance is the doorway to inner peace.

Compassion: Compassion is seeing another's suffering and taking any action to decrease the suffering of others. A smile, a hug, a listening ear or helping hand are all invaluable acts of kindness that brighten up our world and the world for everyone around us. One act of kindness can ripple outward with no logical end. Compassion is when loving kindness meets suffering. Compassion helps us to step outside of our own needs and wants and practice selflessness, putting others first.

Empathetic Joy: Empathetic joy is the opposite of jealously. It is the feeling of experiencing other people's happiness as our own. It is the warmth that fills you when you see a beautiful couple walking past with clasped hands, or a young child opening up a birthday gift. So often in life we are quick to judge or develop jealous feelings for example when a coworker gets a raise and we are left thinking well what about me.

Empathetic joy, however, practices selflessness and experiencing other people's happiness as if it were our own. We can instead rejoice in the good circumstances and situations that others experience instead of comparing them to our own. Everyone in this world suffers and we are all interconnected. What happens to one happens to all. Any good thought, speech or action put into this world makes it a more beautiful place for all of us. Thus, we can practice rejoicing in the happiness of others, and when we do we release negativity and realize that our happiness can have a million sources, instead of just from ourselves.

Equanimity: Equanimity is a calm, stable, balanced, and unshakeable mind. This is the calmness that is cultivated through the practice of meditation. Being equanimous is an important component of loving kindness. There are many situations outside our control including people, places and things. We can and should choose to help to the best of our ability, but after doing your best you have to let go and accept whatever happens. There are some people whom even if you spend your whole life trying to help, will not change.

Equanimity results in stillness and serenity with whatever arises in the mind. This means that you stop clinging to or rejecting certain thoughts, memories or emotions. By cultivating equanimity you'll begin to see the drawbacks of greed, anger and other emotional afflictions, so if they arise in the mind you stay even minded toward them. When you have the mindfulness and wisdom to see the harm in these then you can truly let them go. Equanimity can be equated with resiliency, a person has a strength of mind that is unshakeable despite life stressors.

The Buddha described 4 types of people likened to a lotus flower. One is already blooming on top of the water, going from brightness to brightness. Another is right at the surface and ready to bloom. A third type of lotus is beneath the surface but with time and patience will bloom into the light. The fourth type of lotus is beneath the mud, going from darkness to darkness. No matter how much you try to help this person they will not change. Thus, it is important to balance our compassion with wisdom, to know what is in our power to change and what is not, and let everything else go. It is said that wisdom and compassion are the two wings of a bird that help to keep it balanced and fly. Thus, love yourself and love others but don't forget the middle path. As we meditate daily our lens will be clearer and clearer. The blurriness of our perception directly affects our thoughts, speech, and actions.

Thus, clean your mind every day through daily meditation and maintain the balance between relaxation and mindfulness throughout your day.

Meditation Resources

Beginners find it easiest to listen to a meditation guide or join a class. Below are some free resources for you.

Guided meditations on our book website **www.powersofmeditation.com**

Guided Meditations on Youtube:

Start small and build up. Guided meditations progressive in nature from 5 minutes up to 45 minutes – Meditation Teacher Dawn

Guided Middle Way Meditation & Wisdom Talks - Teaching monk Venerable Nicholas Thanissaro, Ph.D.

2 Part Middle Way Guided Meditation for Beginners - Robert Mawson

PART 1: RELAXATION

PART 2: VISUALIZATION

Self-Development Programs & Sangha

Middle Way Meditation App 'Mindgem' - Meditate and learn wisdom from renowned Buddhist monks around the world. Be a part of a community built on a foundation to scale wisdom and help people find inner happiness. Download the app and learn more at **www.mindgem.org**

42 Day Self Development Program - Make meditation a habit with guided meditations and a personal peace coach.

Sign up at **www.peacerevolution.net**

Join the Meditation Center of Alabama sangha and meet knowledgeable instructors and teaching monks. Gain strength and encouragement from a warm-hearted community of like-minded individuals.

Visit **www.meditationcenteral.com**

CREDITS:

All my understanding and knowledge of meditation was taught and passed down to me by my great teachers. First and foremost, I would like to thank Luang Pu Wat Paknam, founder of the Middle Way Meditation technique, and Luang Phor Dhammajayo, abbot of the Dhammakāya Temple in Thailand. Thank you Venerable Klint Kunachawo and Dawn Barie for helping to review the content of this chapter. I would like to thank each one of my teachers for giving me the greatest gift in the world, the wisdom of how to find true happiness from within. All my wisdom was shared to me and I gift it to you in hopes that you too will be able to find peace and happiness in every step of your life.

5

DHAMMAKĀYA OR "MIDDLE WAY" MEDITATION METHODS

PHRA NICHOLAS THANISSARO, PH.D.

Dhammakāya Meditation

This chapter aims to give context to Dhammakāya meditation, by describing its ancient and modern history, how it fits into the broader picture of meditation techniques, various approaches to its practice, stages of progress along its path, and finally its unique identifying features. In doing this, I have simplified many of the arguments to avoid getting bogged down in Buddhist terminology or academic debate but have included the necessary detail.

ANCIENT ORIGINS

With a history in many ways parallel to the contemporary popularization of the "mindfulness movement," Dhammakāya is a method of meditation that originated from the Buddhist wisdom tradition. However, in the form that has become popular in the Western world, it is often practiced by those who consider themselves neither Buddhist nor religious.

The word dhammakāya means the "embodiment of enlightenment." The term is 2,600 years old, with some detail lost in pre-Theravāda schools of scriptural interpretation. The oldest extant references to Dhammakāya-like meditation methods, focusing on the center of the body, come from the Manual of a Mystic (a Buddhist sub-commentary from the Yogāvacara tradition) and a Dhammakāya inscription found in Phitsanulok, Thailand. Both references place this form of meditation as early as the 16th century. Regardless of how this form of meditation has been perceived by modern reformists and colonial scholars, much evidence points to this form of meditation being accepted as a, if not the, mainstream form of Buddhist practice by monastic and court hierarchy alike, across much of the Theravāda world, before the reforms and Pali canon-based learning of the 19th and 20th centuries.[1]

A MODERN HISTORY

The revival of Dhammakāya meditation in the modern era is attributed to the Thai monk Phramongkolthepmuni (Sodh Candasaro, 1884-1959), who recovered and recombined many elements of borān kammatthāna[2] in a great act of personal sacrifice in 1916 at Wat Boatbon Bangkuvieng, Nonthaburi Province.[3] Having systematized the method, Phramongkolthepmuni taught it to others throughout his life, even establishing a "meditation research workshop" with perpetual meditation reserved for gifted practitioners. Dhammakāya meditation in the second generation has been taught by Phramongkolthepmuni's protégés at several major temples, including Wat Paknam Bhasicharoen and Wat Rajaorasaram in Bangkok, Wat Phra Dhammakāya in Pathum Thani Province, and Wat Luang Por Sodh Dhammakāyaram in Ratchaburi province, as well as in branch centers of these temples in Thailand and abroad.

THE SPECTRUM OF MEDITATION METHODS

Meditation generally refers to methods of focusing the awareness. There are a wide variety of available meditation methods which can be categorized into three broad categories based on where one's awareness is focused. The first category of meditation methods is those that focus the mind outside the body. This group of methods is generally non-Buddhist in origin. Externalizing the mind is easy, because it comes naturally to focus your attention on the world around you. However, such meditation has a drawback in that when meditational vision arises, it tends to be hypnotic and hence misleading. Although for some, the images can be pleasant, for others, they can be frightening. Trance-like states with these meditation methods are not under the practitioner's control, so despite its convenience, such practice is to be discouraged without a dedicated teacher closely on hand.

The second category of meditation methods is those that focus the mind somewhere inside the body, such as the nostril or the heart. Focusing inwardly, the meditator gets the feeling of detachment and equanimity toward the outside world. There is an accompanying experience of inner illumination, quietude, and stillness. This category rarely produces misleading meditational vision because one tends to feel detachment even toward experiences arising in the mind. All that seems to matter are feelings of purity, peace, coolness, and general radiance inside. These will be accompanied by an arising of awareness which is much broader than one has experienced before. While such an experience falls short of the attainment of insight, it does bring relaxation on a certain level.

A third category of meditation methods is those that not only focus inside the body but pinpoint the center of the body specifically. The important place is a point at the center of the diaphragm, a place highlighted as the solar plexus or "abdominal brain" by authors such as Murphy[4] and Dumont.[5] The mind is brought to a state where it is free of thought when focused on this point. When the mind becomes singularly focused on this point, a bright, clear sphere or star will appear in the mind. If the mind is directed continuously at this point, a further level of purity and freedom from mental residue of greed, hatred, and delusion develops. This category of meditations brings not only relaxation but also focus. It is to this third category of meditation methods that Dhammakāya meditation belongs.

DIFFERENT APPROACHES TO DHAMMAKĀYA MEDITATION

Sometimes Dhammakāya meditation is understood to be a single technique, but in fact, it is an approach that can be practiced through a variety of different methods that share the same pathway and goal. There are various methods of getting to the goal: the seven bases, visualizing a picture at the center of the body, feeling (placing the attention at the center of the body without visualizing), observing, mantra repetition, and spreading of loving kindness. Although distinct, all six of the approaches mentioned are in fact ways of focusing the attention at the center of the body, adopted by people of different personality according to their preferences.

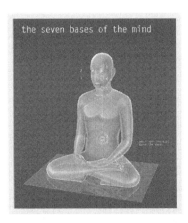

1. Seven Bases Technique

In this method, after relaxing body and mind, a visual (or tactile) object is imagined in front of the face, made smaller, and then moved down through a succession of six points:

1. The nostril (left for females, right for males)
2. Inside the bridge of the nose (left for females, right for males)

3. The center of the skull
4. The palate
5. The Adam's apple
6. The navel

It then reaches the seventh point at the center of the body. This approach is often thought of as an initiation to the center of the body. Having practiced this approach at least once, until the practitioner has familiarized themselves with the position of the seventh point, they can then move on to one of the other methods that start at the seventh point.

2. Visualizing a Picture at the Center

If the meditator prefers to make use of a visual object in their meditation, they can imagine a crystal ball (classically) or any other picture (such as the shining sun) at the center of the body, without needing to move the object through the first six points of technique 1 above. No matter what visual image you start with, later it will become bright, clear, and transparent as the mind becomes more subtle. If the initial image is clear to start with, it takes less time to achieve clarity and transparency in subsequent states of concentration.

3. IMAGINING A TACTILE OBJECT AT THE CENTER

As an alternative to technique 2 above, the meditator can place their attention at the center of the body, feeling that the attention is focused gently on the point where it feels it belongs, without worrying too much if it is exactly at the center of the diaphragm. One might simply rest one's attention at the chosen point or imagine an object there that one can feel (but not see) like the touch of an invisible feather. If the breath is being used, one can focus on the sensation of the breath passing its turning point at the deepest point of the diaphragm, where it stops for an instant between the in-breath and the out-breath. Once the mind comes into equilibrium, the mind will start to move deeper through the center of the body, becoming purer as it goes. This third method will be suitable for meditators who find it impractical to visualize a mental object, perhaps because the act of visualizing makes them feel tense, but who find that the mind wanders without some sort of inner object.

4. MANTRA REPETITION

For this technique of meditation, the meditator silently repeats the sound of a mantra to themselves. A mantra is any short, memorable word or phrase, which is meaningful to you. The default mantra original to the Dhammakāya tradition is "Sammā-Arahaṃ" (which means "a pure state of mind achieved in the proper way"). A more universal mantra might be the phrase "brighter and brighter, clearer and clearer." It should be imagined that the sound of the mantra comes from the center of the body, rather than via your larynx or your ears. This practice can be used in combination with techniques 1-3 above. The mantra is repeated until the thoughts are reduced to a manageable level. Beyond this point, the thoughts can be ignored without returning to the mantra. This approach is particularly necessary for those who have a lot of thoughts on their mind. This approach can be valuable for those whose thoughts keep them awake at night or leave them vulnerable to panic attacks.

5. OBSERVATION

Observation is an approach to Dhammakāya meditation that is like the Zen practice of "just sitting." Instead of conjuring up a visual or tactile object to focus upon in meditation, the meditator merely observes whatever is (already) there to be seen at the center of the body—for example, textures, patterns, or darkness. Even darkness can be considered an object rather than a lack of one. The art of this approach is to suspend judgment while observing. React with neither excitement nor frustration toward whatever arises (or fails to arise) in the mind, nor allow yourself any mental commentary. This technique is good for the more intuitive meditators or those frustrated in their efforts to try to conjure up an object, (techniques 2-3). In practice, techniques 1-4 develop into this method naturally as they advance.

6. Loving Kindness Meditation

Loving kindness meditation is a way to extend and share the inner experience built up by following meditation approaches 1-5. Spreading loving kindness requires the meditator to apply the mind gently at the center of their accumulated inner experience (inner brightness, a feeling of wellbeing or inner imagery) in a way that it melts away from the center and can expand outwards; initially, it fills the whole of the meditator's body (with the accompanying wish "may I be well and happy, may I be free of all suffering"), and then in ever widening circles beyond themselves (with the accompanying wish "may all sentient beings be well and happy, may they be free of all suffering, may they live in peace and harmony"), until reaching out to the entire universe. Being able to practice loving kindness effectively is related to the counter-image or attainment concentration stage of meditation (see stages below). Loving kindness meditation is usually practiced for 5-10 minutes at the end of your regular meditation.

Stages of Progress in Dhammakāya Meditation

When one cultivates meditation continuously, the visual object or state of mind will gradually change in nature in accordance with the increasing subtlety of mind according to the following sequence of three stages. If the meditation technique you are practicing involves an image, you will start out by being able to see a "preparatory image" (parikamma nimitta), which is a vague, partial, or undetailed version of the image you intended to imagine. If one maintains this state of mind gently and continuously, the mental object will change in nature to an "acquired image" (uggaha-nimitta), where you are able to see the image you have imagined with 100% of the clarity and vividness of the external image you based it upon. Once the mind becomes even more free from clouding thoughts or external distractions, so that it is captivated by the image at the center of the body, the image will change to be a "counter image" (patibhāga-nimitta), which the meditator can expand or contract at will. The image will change from a colored image to one that is transparent. For example, if one's previous mental image has been a crystal ball, it will turn into a crystal ball that emits bright radiance and is as light as a bubble, sparkling like a diamond with a brightness equal to the midday sun or brighter.

If the meditation technique you are following involves a feeling or observation, rather than an image, you will need to follow your progress in terms of the quality of your concentration. Meditation will start with a state of "preparatory concentration" (khanika- samādhi), where the mind is still only fleetingly focused. Later, as concentration becomes more stable, it will verge on a threshold state called "neighborhood concentration" (upacāra-samādhi). If one's concentration becomes unified completely with the inner feeling, the quality of concentration will be that of "attainment concentration" (appana-samādhi).

Beyond these stages there are the absorptions, attainment of the "embodiment of enlightenment" (dhammakāya), and the possibility to use the Dhammakāya to practice insight meditation.

CONCLUSION:

Identifying Features of Dhammakāya Meditation

As we have seen, there are different ways to meditate in the Dhammakāya tradition. Although there are different starting points (i.e., different techniques), the trend is for meditation experiences to converge into a more unified experience as meditators proceed along the path. Although there may be diverse starting points, the features that all these methodologies share are use of the center of the body and achievement of a mind free from thought until attaining dhammakāya. These are the goals of Dhammakāya meditation on the level of meditation for calm (samatha). Further down the pathway of Dhammakāya meditation, this platform of "calm" dovetails seamlessly into "insight" (vipassanā) meditation, the description of which is beyond the introductory scope of this chapter.

Further Reading: Dhammakāya Foundation (2004) Start Meditation Today: The Simple Way to Inner Peace. Pathum Thani, Thailand: Dhammakāya Foundation. Earlier editions of this book come with an audio CD that explains how to meditate in the Dhammakāya approach.

---

1. Crosby, K., Skilton, A. & Gunasena, A. (2012). The Sutta on Understanding Death in the Transmission of Borān Meditation from Siam to the Kandyan Court. Journal of Indian Philosophy 40(2): 177-198.

2. Newell, C. S. (2008). Monks, meditation, and missing links: continuity, 'orthodoxy' and the vijjā Dhammakāyain Thai Buddhism. Unpublished PhD dissertation: SOAS, University of London.
3. Dhammakāya_Foundation (2003). The Life & Times of Luang Phaw Wat Paknam. Bangkok: Dhammakāya Foundation.
4. Murphy, J. (2010). The power of your subconscious mind. Mineola, NY: Dover. 29, 68-9
5. Dumont, T. Q. (1920). The solar plexus or abdominal brain. Chicago: Advanced Thought Publishing.

6

THE MANY BENEFITS OF MEDITATION

PART I

M. CAY WELSH, PH.D. AND D. KENT WELSH, PH.D.

Introduction

We began our training to become clinical psychologists more than fifty years ago. Like many young aspiring psychotherapists, we wanted to understand our fellow human beings and to help those who were suffering to recognize the paths to change. We have worked with a variety of patients in many different settings—rape crisis centers, VA hospitals, mental health centers, inpatient psychiatric hospitals, youth offender facilities, university counseling centers, substance abuse treatment centers, correctional facilities, and outpatient psychology offices. We have treated patients who have served in intense combat situations, those who have been victims of violent crime, and those who have lived through unimaginable traumatic childhood abuse. We have encountered patients who have had life-changing accidents and injuries and those with devastating, and sometimes fatal, illnesses.

The work of psychologists may often look easy to the casual observer. After all, don't psychologists just sit and listen to patients, nodding wisely occasionally before sending people on their way? Yet sitting and listening and being fully present with someone, particularly someone in emotional distress, is quite hard and emotionally exhausting. So much so that the psychological profession has recognized a condition called "secondary post trauma syndrome." This is the emotional condition that can occur in therapists and other helpers (health care workers and first responders) whose exposure to people in emotional distress results in empathic emotional distress. The result may lead to a hardening of emotions as well as professional burnout. It may also result in a sense of being overwhelmed by the suffering of others, and creation of anxiety and despair in the helper.

Fortunately for us, our interest in meditation and other strategies to help in management of our own stress began relatively early in our professional careers. Kent first enrolled in a Transcendental Meditation class in the early 1970s while we were still in graduate school. This was during a time of limited financial resources, so the cost of a TM course was a significant hardship. But we continued to meditate individually and together. Later, we became aware of the program of mindfulness meditation developed by Jon Kabat-Zinn that was designed to help people deal with physical and emotional distress. We took several professional training workshops in mindfulness and began incorporating the techniques of mindfulness into our own treatment approaches with patients. We also participated in Buddhist meditation retreats where we learned to recognize the transitory nature of experiences. We learned to step back from our thoughts and emotions, letting them pass without reacting to them. Having learned these skills from meditation helped us to sit fully present and absorb the traumas of our patients without being over-whelmed by our own emotions.

Cay found meditation particularly helpful during times of grief and personal health challenges. While losing one's parents is an expected part of life, it is rarely an unemotional or easy life stage. Having also lost a brother in mid-life made the awareness of our tempo-rary nature more impactful. Meditation lessened the stress and strengthened her awareness of the value of relationships in life's journey. This was particularly comforting when Cay was diagnosed with an aggressive form of breast cancer. It was difficult for her not to dwell on the death of her aunt, who had died at age fifty after having battled cancer for ten years. When faced with serious medical procedures, Cay was fortunate to have understanding physicians who would permit her to listen to meditation tapes while she was being prepped for surgeries or wheeled in for procedures. During Cay's surgery, chemotherapy, and radiation, her daily meditation practice became even stronger than before. She brought meditation tapes to all her chemo treatments, finding meditation to be much more helpful to her personal wellbeing than sitting anxiously for hours or trying to distract herself with the intrusive television programs, as many patients did.

In 2009 Kent saw a hand-written sign offering "Thai Meditation" with an accompanying phone number. When he called it, he was told someone would get back to him. That did not happen until about a year later. When the person on the phone described the meeting time and place, we decided to try it. They found a small group of meditators and were instructed in the Dhammakāya style of meditation. The instruction was given by both Buddhist monks and lay experts in meditation. That small group evolved into a close sangha of people who meditate regularly. This opportunity to meditate with others and to learn more about meditation and Buddhist philosophy have greatly enhanced our understanding and personal practice.

Learning the skills of meditation has helped us in our careers to sit fully present and absorb the traumas of our patients while also noticing our own internal responses. But more importantly, it has helped us in our own private lives and in our personal relationships. We hope that the following chapter can convey a sense of how psychology, meditation, and Buddhist philosophy can be as helpful in your daily life as it has been in ours. After all, learning that we have the power to change our thoughts, our perspectives, and our actions is the ultimate power to change our lives. To see ourselves and others clearly in the interconnection of "all that is" helps build both wisdom and compassion and makes life rich and meaningful.

MEDITATION/MINDFULNESS AND EMOTIONAL HEATH AND WELLBEING

The practice of meditation has ancient roots and has been a part of many religious and cultural traditions. It was well known in India and was emphasized by the Buddha in his teachings circa 500 BCE. While most of the ancient practices originated in Asia with Hindu and Buddhist communities, other forms of meditation were developed in Jewish, Christian, and Islamic cultures.[1] In modern times, meditation was introduced to the Western public as a non-religious practice by the Maharishi Mahesh Yogi, the founder of Transcendental Meditation (TM). The practice gained popularity after the Maharishi taught the Beatles and other celebrities TM. Many young people in the 1960s and '70s participated in this form of meditation. TM is still taught today, and its practices have been included in schools, prisons, and other institutions.[2]

Current Research in Meditation and Mindfulness In the 1980s, Jon Kabat-Zinn became interested in empirically assessing the essential components of meditation and mindfulness. He stripped away the religious components to evaluate the impact of meditation and mindfulness on the physical and emotional health of people. The program he developed is called Mindfulness Based Stress Reduction (MBSR).[3] Since its inception, hundreds of research studies have been published about its use under different conditions and with various populations.

In examining the benefits of meditation on physical and emotional health, psychological researchers have taken two general approaches. One is to study the impact of mindfulness as an adjunctive treatment for individuals who are suffering from clinical levels of physical and emotional distress or disease. Another strategy is to evaluate the changes in mood and well-being in non-clinical populations to determine if there is an enhancement in functioning. In this chapter, we will examine the major research findings from both kinds of psychological research.

Often in clinical research, participants answer self-report questionnaires and keep records of their activities. Other research may also attempt to validate this self-report by gathering some physical measurements such as indicators of stress hormones, blood pressure readings, immune system components, brain wave patterns, etc. All these measures help to evaluate what is going on in the physical body perhaps and reveal the impact of our mental state on physical functioning.

RESEARCH WITH ILLNESS AND DISEASE

Science has demonstrated that many forms of heart disease can be exacerbated by stress. When an individual experiences a stressor, muscle tension increases, blood pressure increases, heart rate increases, and stress hormones are released into the bloodstream as the body prepares for "fight or flight." While this response may have been adaptive in earlier times, in our modern culture, we are seldom confronted with physically threatening situations. Therefore, the "fight or flight" arousal is not burned off by increased activity and the stress hormones continue to circulate causing inflammation and other negative physical conditions. Blood pressure can remain elevated, potentially leading to damage to the heart, blood vessels, and other organs.[4]

Kabat-Zinn's MBSR program addresses these negative physical consequences of stress by teaching individuals' techniques to manage stress. First, the individual is taught to focus attention on a sensation: taste, vision, hearing, etc. The point is to help the person break away from preconceived notions and attend to what is present in the here and now. His definition of mindfulness is "paying attention in a particular way, on purpose, in the present moment and non-judgmentally." Next, the person is taught to scan the body and notice any physical tension. A meditation technique is then introduced, and the person is encouraged to practice the technique on a regular basis. (See Kabat-Zinn's books Mindfulness for Beginners,[5] and Full Catastrophe Living3 for further descriptions of the techniques.)

APPLICATIONS OF MBSR

When Kabat-Zinn began studying meditation and mindfulness, he was working at the University of Massachusetts Medical School. He developed the MBSR program with patients who were combating serious illnesses including cancer, heart disease, and diabetes. The program was conducted in groups of patients with various diagnoses, all participating together. He reasoned that the treatment was a general treatment and not specific to any disorder or disease. Since its inception, MBSR has been applied to numerous populations, including patients with various chronic diseases as well as people dealing with environmental, social, and personal stress.

It has been well documented that stress tends to shorten one's life span. Selye[6] demonstrated the negative effect of stress on rats during experiments conducted in the 1950s, and thousands of studies in humans have also shown the deleterious effects of stress on our health. One impact of chronic stress is an acceleration of the aging process. At the chromosomal level, one measure of aging is reflected by the length of telomeres. A telomere is a small cap on the end of each chromosome. Each time a cell divides, the telomeres on its chromosomes become shorter. After numerous divisions, the telomeres become too short, thus losing information needed for accurate cell division. At this point, the cell dies or divides in a more random manner, a condition that can lead to mutations or unhealthy cells. The good news is that the body can lengthen telomeres through the action of the enzyme telomerase. Anything that enhances production of telomerase can potentially increase the number of times a cell divides, hence increasing its healthy reproduction.

There are some lifestyle factors that have been shown to be beneficial to maintaining the length of one's telomeres. First, reduce and control stress. MBSR is specifically designed for this purpose. Meditation alone has been shown to increase telomerase activity. Regular meditation appears to slow the process of telomere shortening and increase the lifespan of cells. The precise mechanism is still not completely known, but the results so far are promising.

The body's immune system is its defense against pathogens that cause disease. In a 2016 article in the journal Biological Psychiatry, the authors examined the role of mindfulness meditation in moderating the immune response.[7] They concluded that when practiced regularly, mindfulness meditation possibly has a positive effect of reducing inflammation and increasing immune cell production. The authors encouraged further research in this area.

EMOTIONAL BENEFITS

While the mind is an elusive concept, the brain, as a physical organ, plays a major role in our thoughts, perceptions, and feelings. Consequently, neuroscientists with the use of modern imaging tools, such as fMRI (functional Magnetic Resonance Imaging), have been documenting which areas of the brain are associated with specific mood states and thought patterns. A recurring finding is that most people's brains, when they have nothing else to think about, focus on a negative, self-referencing thought pattern.[8] How did neuroscientists identify this distressing pattern of thought? Participants in brain imaging studies using fMRI were simply asked to "not think about anything" while their brains were being scanned. What the researchers found was that, instead of neural activity slowing down, it increased. Specifically, activity increased in areas of the brain associated with worry, anxiety, and negative self-evaluation. Researchers have dubbed this pattern as "the negative default state of the brain." That is, our "natural" way of experiencing ourselves is by ruminating over past mistakes or failures, anticipating future disasters and threats, and assessing ourselves negatively compared to others. No wonder many of us seek to distract ourselves from just being with ourselves.

Interestingly, when researchers examined the brain activity of meditators who practiced regularly, this "negative default state" was not prominent. Apparently, the practice of meditation teaches the brain different patterns of thinking and feeling. The meditators learn to observe their thoughts, rather than "get caught up in them," and they learn to observe their feelings rather than be overwhelmed by them. This practice of repeatedly observing thoughts, feelings, and sensations, and letting them go and redirecting attention to a simple awareness in the present, changes not only how our brain functions but changes the structure of the brain itself. Research has demonstrated that the brain develops new neural pathways from the frontal cortex to the limbic system when meditation is practiced regularly.[9] Thus, the "higher" or more reasoned part of our brain is able to send calming or inhibitory signals to the more primitive, reactive, and emotional parts of the brain. How does this finding apply to the actual emotional difficulties that people may experience? In the following section we will summarize the major findings of meditation/mindfulness as a component of treatment for emotional difficulties.

DEPRESSION

Depression is a common difficulty in our society, and, despite the prosperity of the modern world, the rate of depression appears to be increasing rather than decreasing. Depression is different from sadness, which is a normal, reactive response, typically to unfortunate events. It is differentiated from depression by the extent to which the negative mood impacts many aspects of our functioning and the subjective experience of feeling stuck and overwhelmed by the negative mood. When depression is severe it interferes with our ability to think, to interact with others, to sleep normally, to eat appropriately, to plan, to work, or even to want to live.

While relatively short-term depression is common, some individuals experience recurrent episodes of depression that are particularly difficult to overcome. Psychologists have found that teaching depressed individuals' skills to notice, to evaluate, and to modify their negative thought patterns is an effective means of treating depression. These strategies are a component of Cognitive Behavior Therapy (CBT). However, with recurrent depression, patients often become discouraged, thinking that "nothing really works for long" and "all is hopeless" regarding their prospects for getting better.[10]

The addition of mindfulness training to cognitive behavior therapy, particularly for recurrent depression, has led to more effective outcomes for those suffering from recurrent depression. One benefit of meditation is the experience and self-knowledge that "everything is temporary." Our thoughts change: they come and go. Our feelings modify, they increase, they decrease, they morph into another experience. Our perceptions change as well; we can notice our experiences from a different perspective. When a new wave of depression appears, rather than experiencing the recurrence as a failure, or an indication of never getting better, the meditator has the skills to recognize the first symptoms of depression. They can remember the techniques that have been helpful before and allow themselves to simply be supportive until the depression passes. While this is not easily achieved, the research indicates that, with continued practice, meditation is an effective component of treatment for recurrent depression.

Experiencing uncomfortable emotions is a normal (and vital) part of living. By attempting to squelch or avoid our difficult emotions, we can make the problem worse; or we can cut ourselves off from other more positive emotions, leaving ourselves feeling numb and empty. Mindful awareness of our feelings can help us identify the sources of our emotions, can aid us in responding to our feelings more adaptively, and can give us insight and understanding of ourselves and our circumstances. We can notice where in our body we experience certain emotions. Is it in our chest, our gut, our muscle tension, a lump in our throat, a fluttering in our heartbeat, etc.? We can notice what thoughts are associated with those sensations or feelings. We can also begin to practice mental "meteorology." Just as clouds come and go, weather fronts come and go and seasons come and go, our mental states, thoughts, feelings, and perceptions appear, build, transform, diminish, and become another experience. Thus, we can learn the skills of letting go and not getting stuck and overwhelmed by our own thoughts and emotions.

ANXIETY

Another difficult emotion for many people is anxiety.[11] Anxiety has many varieties, but it generally involves an excessive fear or discomfort about some negative event that could happen to us in the future. Anxiety is often accompanied by arousal of the sympathetic nervous system and the generally uncomfortable sensations of rapid heartbeat, difficulty breathing, increased perspiration, dry mouth, muscle tension, trembling, and the urge to escape or run away from the situation.

Fear and anxiety likely developed in humans as a warning system to alert us to potential danger. If we can spot potential danger soon enough, perhaps we can avoid it. Many of us may find ourselves drawn to news of disasters and misfortunes, and we can often be bombarded with information of catastrophes from around the world in such a way that we live in a state of perpetual worry and pessimism. While certainly negative events do occur, we often spend little time focusing on the positive events that are also happening. Meditation helps us to learn to sit with our thoughts, feelings, and sensations as they occur and to be aware that these internal events will transform. By staying with them in the safety of the present moment, we can interrupt the mind's tendency to "jump forward" into the realm of imagined disaster. By its very nature, anxiety is anticipatory. It is the "what if" anticipation of disaster that captures our mind in the quicksand of anxiety. The more we struggle with "not thinking about" or avoiding the thoughts that frighten us, the stronger the fears can grab hold of us. The skills of meditation allow us to notice our thoughts, sensations, and emotions as they occur. Meditation gives us the experience of "impermanence"—that all things change, and nothing remains the same forever, including our own discomfort. It will eventually abate. Our body physiology will return to baseline, our heart rate and breathing will normalize, our muscles will begin to relax, etc.

There are times when anxiety takes the form of worry. A benefit of projecting our imagination into the future is that it can help us anticipate possible problems and then generate alternative solutions and courses of action. It is important to recognize that the process of planning is adaptive. However, worry is going over the same scenarios and anticipating the same negative outcomes. Worry can even give us the illusion that we are doing "something" in the face of a potential problem. So often we can get in the habit of worrying about our health, our family, our job, our relationships, and our finances, believing that by worrying we are somehow preventing the negative outcomes. In the meantime, our bodies respond to these "what if" events as if they are happening. So, we end up depleting our mental and emotional energy and creating physical distress in our bodies, thus negatively impacting our health.

Meditation can allow us to practice a form of psychological treatment for anxiety that is called exposure and response prevention. In this type of treatment, an individual is exposed to or experiences the situation that elicits fear or anxiety but is not allowed to escape from the situation. Gradually, the emotional arousal dissipates, and, with repeated exposure, the anxiety response becomes less and "extinguishes." In meditation, we can learn to notice our own frightening thoughts or worries, our uncomfortable sensations of anxiety, and sit with them until they abate or transform. This form of psychological treatment is very effective with phobias and anxiety.

ANGER

Anger is another difficult emotion for many people in our society. It has different variations—sometimes it manifests as irritation, impatience, or criticism and judgment. It can be intense and violent and have very negative consequences. In some way, anger involves wanting something or someone to be different than they are. It may be that something we want has been blocked from us and we are frustrated with the outcome. Oftentimes, it is our own selves that we are frustrated with, and we are judging ourselves negatively and wanting to be different than we are. As with other difficult emotions, research has shown that people can learn through meditation practice to begin to modify their reactions and responses to situations that would have previously aroused anger. By being aware of the responses of our physical body sooner, by noticing our thoughts and letting them go, we can begin to soothe and calm ourselves until our thoughts and responses transform and subside. We may be able to gain insight into the origins of our anger and the various factors that may be playing a role in our angry response. Perhaps we are tired, hungry, or in pain. Or perhaps the current situation is reminiscent of an event that has happened to us before, and our response mirrors that event rather than what is occurring at this time. Meditation can help us to develop a sense of patience with ourselves and others that can allow anger to dissipate more quickly.

OTHER DIFFICULT EMOTIONS AND MEDITATION AS A HEALTHIER COPING MECHANISM

The same strategies for responding to depression, anxiety, and anger can also be applied to other common uncomfortable emotions. Thich Nhat Hahn, a noted Zen master, suggests dealing with difficult emotions by personifying them, perhaps by imagining the feelings as a small child and offering to breathe and sit with them.[12] For example, one might address a feeling in this way: "Hello, anger. I know you. Come sit on my lap. I will breathe with you and sit with you until you are better." This practice takes away the struggle and judgment of our own emotions and allows the emotions to naturally transform. Similarly, Thich Nhat Hahn states that, "If we know how to grieve, we grieve less." This practice acknowledges that our emotions are normal, even the uncomfortable ones, and that giving them attention and compassion allows the emotions to run their natural course more quickly. Grief is a normal human response to the loss of someone or something that is important to us. Denying our grief can prolong the recovery process. Giving ourselves permission to notice and experience our grieving without judgment, yet with compassion and kindness, allows the healthy transformation of grief into acceptance and wisdom.

Mindfulness has also been incorporated into treatment programs for substance abuse, eating disorders, and behavioral disorders such as gambling or compulsive shopping. The primary focus for treatment in these disorders is to use mindfulness to both prevent avoidance of difficult emotions and to help the person learn to notice the first cues that the problematic response may be triggered. Often, unhealthy behavioral responses such as drinking, drugging, and gambling are attempts to numb our emotions or to distract us from our difficult feelings. By teaching the skills of breathing, noticing the body, and stepping back from our thoughts and feelings and simply observing them, we give ourselves the opportunity to make a different, healthier, wiser choice. A famous saying often attributed to Victor Frankl, a famous psychiatrist and holocaust survivor, is "Between the stimulus and the response there is a gap. In that gap is your power to choose your response." By stepping back not only from environmental cues that may prompt poor choices, but also from our own internal states, we can learn to observe with equanimity and curiosity what our own mind generates without getting too reactive or ensnared by our own mental turmoil.

BENEFITS IN RELATIONSHIPS

Just as mindfulness and meditation skills can be beneficial to individuals' wellbeing and happiness, it has also been proven to be beneficial in interpersonal interactions. Numerous studies have demonstrated an improvement in communication and in positive interactions following the regular practice of mindfulness with couples in marital therapy and in groups of couples who are wanting to enhance their relationships.

Specific programs have been developed that have modified Kabat-Zinn's MBSR (Mindfulness Based Stress Reduction) format to Mindfulness Based Relationship Enhancement (MBRE).[13] This adaptation is typically taught in eight weekly sessions, including a full day weekend retreat during the sixth week. These programs are designed for couples who are seeking enhanced relationships rather than for distressed couples. The techniques focus specifically on using mindfulness skills in communications, so that one can more accurately hear and respond to one's partner. Additionally, MBRE incorporates use of practices such as loving kindness meditation aimed at our partner's wellbeing.

These programs may also include mindful couples' yoga practice and mindful touch exercises. Some programs utilize an exercise of gazing into their partner's eyes for an extended period, noticing their own responses, and recognizing the "deep-down goodness" present in their partners and in themselves. These exercises are designed to help couples become more aware and supportive of their shared pleasant activities as well as aware of stressful interaction and how to develop new understandings of themselves and their partners. MBRE differs from traditional marital enhancement programs by emphasizing a single skill: that of bringing non-judgmental awareness to one's on-going, in-the-moment, experiences. This approach focuses on greater acceptance of self, of partner, and of life circumstances, as well as greater calmness of body and mind and greater feelings of love and connectedness. Research studies confirm that couples who participate in MBRE show dramatic changes in acceptance of partner, average daily relationship happiness, and a decrease in average daily relationship stress. Positive change has also been shown in feelings of autonomy and relatedness, along with feelings of relaxation, spirituality, and optimism. These improvements were maintained when follow-up measures were taken three months post treatment.

Thich Nhat Hahn advises that nothing can grow if it is not watered, and he includes relationships in that observation. He encourages couples to view their partner as a lovely flower that needs regular watering to grow, or the love within will wither and not prosper.[14] His concept of "watering a relationship" includes using loving and kind speech and letting the other person know what we appreciate about them.

PARENTING

Mindfulness parenting skills can be very important in improving interactions between parents and children. Young children look to their parents' emotional responses in a situation to gauge their own responses. Parents who are stressed themselves are often easily frustrated and unable to respond effectively to the complex demands of parenting. This can lead to a spiral of negative emotional responses between the parent and child. Effective parenting includes many mindfulness related skills. It is difficult but important to learn to not take our child's behavior personally. A child's misbehavior or difficult moods are prompted by many events, and we are not responsible for our child's reactions. Using the mindfulness skills of stepping back from a situation, observing non-judgmentally with a moment-to-moment awareness, can allow us to respond more effectively to whatever a child does. Sometimes, a small child having a temper tantrum may need a nap, or perhaps they are hungry. They may be getting ill or need to be held. They may even need for the parent to walk away and allow the tantrum to run its course. It takes a wise parent looking deeply into the situation to discern which response may be most needed in a particular circumstance. The mindfulness skills of breathing, calming oneself, and developing equanimity are helpful in parenting skills. For further information, see Dr. Dan Siegel's book on mindful parenting[15] and the book by Myla and Jon Kabat-Zinn, Everyday Blessings: The Inner Work of Mindful Parenting.[16]

SOCIETAL APPLICATIONS

There have been many programs developed to bring mindfulness skills into societal organizations such as school systems. These programs have demonstrated that children can enhance their emotional intelligence and learn better stress management techniques[17] through mindfulness practice. Mindfulness has also been utilized in schools as a counter to bullying, and to enhance kindness and cooperation. It has even been used to help children with ADHD to develop better focus and concentration.

For additional applications of mindfulness in societal organizations, see A Mindful Nation, written by US congressman Tim Ryan. In this book, he concludes that the utilization of mindfulness meditation could have an important impact on virtually every aspect of our society.[18]

POSITIVE EFFECTS OF MEDITATION IN THE WORKPLACE

The tech companies of Silicon Valley attract bright, ambitious individuals who are often competing with people in their own company as well as with other companies to produce innovative and profitable technology. The intensity of the competition and the demands for performance can be overwhelming. Workplace stress is common for many people in our society, as focus on output and profitability are increasingly emphasized. Worker's report experiencing work related stress, burnout, and health distress related to their jobs.

Chade-Meng Tan, a former software engineer at Google, developed a program for employees at Google that has now spread to other corporations and organizations. His 2012 book *"Search Inside Yourself"*[19] humorously describes his program of teaching meditation and mindfulness. He emphasizes the positive effects that can be achieved by learning and practicing these techniques on a regular basis. In the book, Tan cites examples of employees who learned to be more mindful and how it changed their approach to their jobs, their coworkers, and their families. As people become more mindful in their interactions with others, they are better able to listen and understand other people. Their level of empathy increases, and they connect with others on a deeper level. Conflicts are reduced as people interact more calmly.

Additional benefits Cade-Meng describes are greater creativity and improved problem solving. When people are not locked into previous ways of thinking, they can see new and different solutions to problems. The ability to monitor one's emotions and step back from them is one aspect of mindfulness. As we tune our "high resolution perception," we notice the changes in our body as an emotion is beginning and trace its trajectory from start to finish. By noticing and labeling the emotion at an early stage in its development, we can moderate its expression in our behavior.

Conclusions

The ancient practices of mindfulness and meditation have been shown in modern times to have many health and emotional benefits. It has been demonstrated that the practice of meditation modifies physical structures in our cells and our brains, and that it enhances our health and wellbeing. Meditation is relatively simple to learn, even by children and adolescents, can be helpful to individuals and couples, and is useful in school settings and in workplaces.

While meditation is not a substitute for medical or mental health treatment, it is a beneficial adjunctive procedure and enhances the functioning and wellbeing of healthy individuals. Meditation can be introduced into even a busy person's life with individual practice sessions. Joining a meditation group or sangha promotes further social support and enhancement of the meditation experience.

---

1. Mitchell, D. W. (2002). Buddhism: Introducing the Buddhist Experience (2nd Ed.) Oxford: Oxford University Press.
2. Roth, B. (2018). Strength in Stillness. New York: Simon & Schuster.
3. Kabat-Zinn, J. (1990) Full Catastrophe Living. New York: Delacorte Press.
4. Sapolsky, R. (1998) Why Zebras Do Not Get Ulcers. New York: W. H. Freeman Publishers
5. Kabat-Zinn, J. (2006) Mindfulness for Beginners. Audiobook. Boulder, CO: Sounds True Publishers.
6. Selye, H. (1976) Stress in Health and Disease. London: Butterworth-Heinemann Publishers.
7. Cresswell, J.D., Taren, A.A., Lindsay, E.K., Greco, C.M., Gianaros, P.J., Fairguene, A., Marsland, A.L., Brown, K.W., Way, B.M., Rosen, R.K. & Farris, J.K. (2016) Alteration in Resting State Functional Connectivity Link Mindfulness Meditation with Reduced Interleukin6: A Randomized Control Trial. Biological Psychiatry, 80(1), 53-61.
8. Buchner, R. L., Andrews-Hanna, J.R., & Schacter, D.L. (2008). The Brain's Default Network: Anatomy, Function, and Relevance to Disease. Annals of the New York Academy of Science, 123(1), 1-38.

9. Hanson, R. (2013) Hardwiring Happiness: The New Brain Science of Contentment, Calm and Confidence. New York: Harmony Books.

10. William, M., Teasdale, J., Segal, Z., & Kabat-Zinn, J. (2007). The Mindful Way Through Depression: Freeing Yourself from Chronic Unhappiness. New York: Guildford Press.

11. Baer, R.A. (2006). Mindfulness Based Treatment Approaches: Clinician's Guide to Evidence Base and Applications. Burlington, MA: Academic Press.

12. Hahn, Thich Nhat (2001). Anger: Wisdom for Cooling the Flames. New York: Riverhead Books

13. Carson, J.W., Carson, K.M., Gil, K.M., & Baucom, D. H. (2006). Mindfulness Based Relationship Enhancement (MBRE) in Couples. In Ruth, A.B. (Ed.), Mindfulness Based Treatment Approaches. Burlington, MA: Academic Press.

14. Hahn, Thich Nhat (2007). How to Love. Berkeley, CA: Parallax Press

15. Siegel, D. & Hartzell, M (2003). Parenting from the Inside Out. New York: Penguin Press.

16. Kabat-Zinn, M, & Kabat-Zinn, J. (1997). Everyday Blessings: The Inner Work of Mindful Parenting. New York: Hyperion Press.

17. Lantieri, L & Goleman, D. (2014). Building Emotional Intelligence Practice to Cultivate Inner Resilience in Children. Boulder, CO: Sounds True Press.

18. Ryan, Tim. (2012). A Mindful Nation. New York: Hay House Publishers.

19. Tan, Chade-Meng (2012). Search Inside Yourself: The Unexpected Path to Achieving Success, Happiness (and World Peace). New York: Harper-Collins Press.

7

THE MANY BENEFITS OF MEDITATION
PART II

PHRA NICHOLAS THANISSARO, PH.D.

EVIDENCE-BASED BENEFITS OF MEDITATION

Despite some recent detractors,[1] the general consensus is that there is a significant and reliable body of evidence that meditation has broadly beneficial effects for practitioners.[2] In this chapter, I would like to highlight four levels at which research evidence has shown benefits brought by meditation: brain physiology, clinical, personality, and society. Most of the benefits discussed here are applicable to meditation techniques in general, although benefits specific to Dhammakāya meditation are also mentioned where available. Some of the studies on meditation in the 1970s were problematic, such as having too few subjects or not being randomly controlled trials, but these problems have been rectified in more recent studies.

BRAIN PHYSIOLOGY

When meditators talk about the mind, they usually mean the "awareness" rather than the brain; but there are places where awareness and brain function overlap. Recent advances in brain neurophysiology, particularly the fMRI scan, have allowed activity of the brain to be monitored in live human subjects and have shown that the brain experiences several demonstrable advantages from regular meditation practice. Contrary to the assumption that brain development stops after child-hood and deteriorates from young adulthood onwards, brain changes linked with meditation show meditators can, to their advantage, exploit the phenomenon of neuroplasticity to continue rewiring their own brains throughout their lifetime.

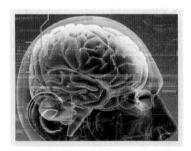

GENERAL WEAKNESSES IN THE BRAIN

Our brains have several inbuilt weaknesses that render us disproportionately sensitive to suffering in life. Owing to survival adaptations that are a throwback to prehistoric times, when the brain scans for stimulation it tends to ignore happiness and instead registers, recalls, and reacts preferentially to unpleasant experiences. Negative experiences are stored indelibly in the hippocampus. Even a single episode of depression can reshape circuits of the brain to make future episodes more likely.[3] Suffering cascades into the body via the sympathetic nervous system (SNS), causing reflexive "fight or flight" responses.

The prefrontal cortex (PFC), anterior grey matter of the frontal lobe, plays a role in the rational regulation of emotional functioning. Failings of the PFC include rehearsal of negativity[4] and failure to control negative impulses. Thinning of the PFC is associated with depression and memory loss. The limbic system is a complex system of nerves and networks in the brain linked to instinct and mood. It aids in the regulation of reflexive emotions and drives, but often fails to do this. The anterior cingulate cortex (ACC) appears to play a role in compassionate emotion.

ADVANTAGES OF A MEDITATIONAL LIFESTYLE

Through meditation, the "rational" PFC can be trained to control the "emotional" limbic system. Meditation was linked with increased blood flow in the PFC[5] and cortical thickening,[6] suggesting that meditation might offset age-related thinning of the cortex associated with depression and offer an alternative way to avoid or roll back depression that usually requires coaching, psychotherapy, or medication.[7]

Since meditators have been shown to be more in touch with their subconscious urges than others,[8] by implication they have more chance to catch and control urges before they lead to damaging behavior. This is certainly true of meditators' enhanced ability to control SNS fight or flight reflexes, since there is evidence to show that long-term meditation can train a person to startle less at loud noises.[9] Meditation also increases blood flow to the thalamus,[10] which is associated with higher cognitive processing. Meditative expertise seems to enhance compassionate emotions by stimulating the ACC.[11] Meditation is associated with increased grey matter concentration in the regions of the brain involved in learning and memory processes, emotion regulation, self-referential processing, and perspective taking.[12]

Often the extreme reactions we must negative circumstances in our lives have a worse impact on our wellbeing than the circumstances themselves. Meditation makes a person less susceptible to these reactions. Apart from stimulating increased blood flow to beneficial parts of the brain, meditation also seems to affect the brain positively through the patterns of brainwaves it produces. Meditation is known to synchronize powerful gamma brainwaves. Similarly, non-directive meditation increases theta and alpha brainwaves, brain activity usually associated with wakeful, relaxed attention rather than merely with brain downtime.[13] In conclusion, meditation provides more balanced brain functioning.

CLINICAL BENEFITS OF MEDITATION

Moving on from the benefits of meditation seen in brain physiology, it appears that meditation can help overcome several clinical conditions that diminish our subjective wellbeing. Research shows meditation to be a good alternative therapy for stress, depression, sleep disorders, and other health conditions.

Meditation has been shown to reduce stress. Dhammakāya meditation, like other methods of meditation,[14] is linked with reduction of physiological indicators of stress, such as serum cortisol levels and high blood pressure. Pulse rate and maximal voluntary ventilation were also reduced.[15] More general research on mindfulness shows promise for meditation as an alternative treatment of PTSD.[16] Dhammakāya meditation has also been shown effective in treating clinical depression,[17] especially where depression has been triggered by a pessimistic outlook on the world. More generally, meditation has been shown to reduce the risk of depression relapse.[18]

On the subject of sleep disorders, it has been shown that long-term meditators may need less sleep than the average person,[19] and that meditation can provide an effective treatment for insomnia, with benefits sustained even over a six-month period.[20]

Other aspects of health where meditation has shown to be beneficial include chronic pain, where a recent review of 22 studies concluded that acceptance-based interventions such as meditation have small to medium beneficial effects on physical and mental health of chronic pain patients.[21] There have been a number of cases of cancer regression following intensive meditation, even in the absence of orthodox medical treatment.[22] Serum cholesterol levels were significantly reduced in those who practiced meditation regularly for a year,[23] and meditation has also proved a useful adjunct in treating asthma.[24] A review of 36 studies showed the efficacy of meditation in reducing the symptoms of anxiety.[25] If practiced regularly, meditation may help prevent coronary heart disease, myocardial infarction and re-infarction,[26] and meditation can be effective in helping to reduce the frequency and severity of migraine attacks.[27] Meditation may even help keep us young. Standard tests of biological aging including auditory threshold, near point vision, and systolic blood pressure measured meditators to be, on average, 2.2 years "younger" than their expected age ratings![28]

BENEFITS OF MEDITATION FOR THE PERSONALITY

Evidence shows that meditation helps with happiness and positive affect, personality and self-esteem, self-actualization, empathy, spirituality, and enhanced learning ability. Meditation can help a person change from reliance on external conditions (which are beyond their control) to conditions inside themselves (which are more under their control) to make them happier. Frequent meditators reported a significantly higher level of positive affect and lower levels of anxiety, hostility, and dysphoria.[29] Meditators showed more improvement on measures of happiness when compared to subjects following a Personal Happiness Enhancement Program who did not meditate.[30]

Meditation plays a role in enhancing personality and self-esteem, leading people closer to reaching their personal goals. Regular meditators become more settled and satisfied with their responsibilities, and more patient and accepting of the things beyond their control. Research on the connection between Dhammakāya meditation and character building[31] has shown that a range of character virtues are perceived more clearly in practitioners as they accumulate more experience in meditation, and meditators generally have a more positive perception of their behavior.[32] Increased self-esteem was found in meditators, even amongst those with chronic illnesses such as HIV-positive men.[33] Meditation increased overall self-esteem, feelings of worth, benevolence, and self-acceptance in those who had participated in only a seven-day meditation retreat.[34] Meditation was found to be associated with an overall increase in measures of positive personality growth.[35]

Meditation has been shown to enhance self-actualization, which means "becoming the best version of yourself." Meditators were found to score significantly more positive than non-meditators in terms of self-concept, as measured on the Tennessee Self-concept Scale.[36] The more people meditated, the more they came to perceive their actual selves as being similar to their ideal and social-selves.[37] A review of 42 studies found significant improvement in self-actualization as a result of meditation.[38] On a personal orientation inventory, those who had meditated for ten weeks had significantly higher scores on inner-directed and time competence scales.[39] Those who meditated also had higher levels of self-esteem, satisfaction, ego-strength, self-actualization, and trust in others.[40]

Meditation helps in the development of empathy, to the extent that participating in meditation for eight weeks helped meditators identify expressions of faces in photographs with improved empathetic accuracy.[41] Increased levels of empathy were found in meditating students,[42] and even a single session of meditation has been shown to reduce indices of anger in experienced and novice meditators alike.[43] Meditation was found to be associated with becoming more open-minded, as defined by the Rokeach Dogmatism Scale.[44] College undergraduates who meditated attained significant gains in creativity.[45] The qualities of having a sense of basic trust, openness, and caring (also known as "affiliative trust"), and having a positive sense of being part of something larger than oneself (also known as "oneness motivation"), have been shown to increase over the course of a mindfulness intervention.[46] Meditation also helped with proficiency in solving interpersonal problems.[47] Meditation has also been associated with a deepened sense of spirituality, supported by studies which have shown that significantly higher scores than average were obtained on a measure of spiritual experience in a group of undergraduate students who had learned meditation.[48] Readers should note, however, that in some cases mindfulness and meditation have been commercialized and banalized to the point that they have become nothing more than a secularized "therapy," a so-called "McMindfulness," with a reduced potential to stimulate any connection with spirituality.[49]

Studies indicate that meditation enhances learning abilities.[50] The association between meditation, learning, and intelligence can perhaps be explained by the way meditation seems to enhance memory and accelerate knowledge acquisition.[51] In elementary schools, mindfulness practice has been shown to help with cognitive outcomes, socio-educational skills, and well-being of pupils.[52] Meditation in public schools and universities was associated with significantly higher grades.[53] Meditation also seemed to improve cognitive flexibility in the elderly. [54]

SOCIAL BENEFITS OF MEDITATION

The final category of benefits to be examined in this chapter is the prevention and cure of social problems. Meditation's links to social wellbeing are based on the idea that society is the sum of the individual parts that comprise it. The more people in any society who learn to meditate and live peacefully, the more that shared "endemic" problems like crime and drug abuse will be diminished. On a more metaphysical level, practicing meditation helps to roll back unwholesome influences in the world. It should be admitted that on this level, the benefits of meditation are harder to prove, and less research is available.

Meditation has been shown to help with rehabilitation of prison inmates, evidenced by a meditation intervention at Folsom State Prison in California, where prisoners trained in meditation showed decreased anxiety, neuroticism, resentment, negativism, irritability, hostility, and prison disciplinary rule infractions.[55] Incorporating meditation into the lifestyle of individuals recovering from addiction provides a consistent means of preparing for inevitable addiction-related life challenges.[56] Meditation has also been shown to help reduce alcohol abuse.[57]

The social implications of meditation were examined in a study which showed that long-term meditators, more than short-term meditators, were significantly less socially withdrawn, more positive in their outlook on human nature, more sociable, and had less pronounced feelings of social inadequacy.[58] There have been movements toward a consciousness-based approach to peace, such as the Global Peace Initiative pioneered mostly by Transcendental Meditation (TM), which arranged for 4000 expert meditators to meditate together in Washington D.C. in 1993. This meditation event coincided with a 23% reduction in crime in the D.C. area. The goal of TM events was to "achieve a critical mass of higher awareness through a unified field precipitating a shift in consciousness."[59] Similar approaches have been applied to reduce the "collective tension" precipitating terrorism, international conflict,[60], and political violence.[61]

Many people were outraged when philosopher Ken Wilbur claimed that "the best way to stop famine in the world is to meditate." However, when Joachim Chissano, became president of Mozambique, at the end of a fifteen-year long civil war that had left millions of dead, he also had the chance to learn how to meditate. Rather than trying to shore up his own power by enacting revenge on rebel forces, he compromised, rescuing almost three million people from extreme poverty from 1997 to 2003. Chissano's rationality and compassion as a leader, alleviating poverty and healing a broken country, is attributed to his commitment to meditation.[62] It is notable that Chissano did not meditate alone, but required his family, government ministers, police, and army to meditate too, twice a day for twenty minutes.

FURTHER READING:

Hanson, R. (2009) Buddha's Brain: the practical neuroscience of happiness, love, and wisdom. Oakland, CA: New Harbinger. A book which explains how, through meditation and mindfulness, the idealized brain can be attained – and linking with selected Buddhist teachings.

Shapiro, S.L., Schwartz G.E.R and Santerre, C. (2002) 'Meditation and Positive Psychology'. In Snyder, C.R., and Lopez S.J. (eds.) Handbook of Positive Psychology, pp.632-645. A chapter which gives an overview of research from the era 1965-1982 on the benefits of meditation to personality.

---

1. Van Dam, N. T., van Vugt, M. K., Vago, D. R., Schmalzl, L., Saron, C. D., Olendzki, A., Meissner, T., Lazar, S. W., Kerr, C. E., Gorchov, J., Fox, K. C. R., Field, B. A., Britton, W. B., Brefczynski-Lewis, J. A. & Meyer, D. E. (2018). Mind the Hype: A Critical Evaluation and Prescriptive Agenda for

Research on Mindfulness and Meditation. Perspectives on Psychological Science, 13(1): 36-61. doi:10.1177/1745691617709589

2. Hofmann, S. G., Grossman, P. & Hinton, D. E. (2011). Loving-kindness and compassion meditation: Potential for psychological interventions. Clinical Psychology Review, 31 1126-1132.

3. Maletic, V., Robinson, M., Oakes, T., Iyengar, S., Ball, S. G. & Russell, J. (2007). Neurobiology of Depression: An Integrated View of Key Findings. International Journal of Clinical Practice, 61 2030-2040.

4. Gusnard, D. A., Abuja, E., Schulman, G. I. & Raichle., M. E. (2001). Medial prefrontal cortex and self-referential mental activity: Relation to a default mode of brain function. Proceedings of the National Academy of Sciences, 984259-4264.

5. Newberg, A. B., Wintering, N., Waldman, M. R., Amen, D., Khalsa, D. S. & Alavi, A. (2010). Cerebral blood flow differences between long-term meditators and non-meditators. Consciousness and Cognition, 19(4): 899-905.

6. Lazar, S. W., Kerr, C. E., Wasserman, R. H., Gray, J. R., Greve, D. N., Treadway, M. T., McGarvey, M., Quinn, B. T., Dusek, J. A., Benson, H., Rauch, S. L., Moore, C. I. & Fischl, B. (2005). Meditation experience is associated with increased cortical thickness. NeuroReport, 16(17): 1893-1897.

7. Peterson, B. S., Warner, V., Bansal, R., Zhu, H., Hao, X., Liu, J., Durkin, K., Adams, P. B., Wickramaratne, P. & Weissman, M. M. (2009). Cortical thinning in persons at increased familial risk for major depression. Proceedings of the National Academy of Sciences, 106(15): 6273-6278.

8. Lush, P., Naish, P. & Dienes, Z. (2016). Metacognition of intentions in mindfulness and hypnosis. Neuroscience of Consciousness, 2016(1): niw007.

9. Levenson, R. W. E., Paul; Ricard, Matthieu (2012). Meditation and the startle response: A case study. Emotion, 12(3): 650-658

10. Newberg, A. B., Wintering, N., Waldman, M. R., Amen, D., Khalsa, D. S. & Alavi, A. (2010). Cerebral blood flow differences between long-term meditators and non-meditators. Consciousness and Cognition, 19(4): 899-905.

11. Lutz, A., Brefczynski-Lewis, J., Johnstone, T. & Davidson, R. J. (2008). Regulation of the Neural Circuitry of Emotion by Compassion Meditation: Effects of Meditative Expertise. PLoS ONE, 3(3): e1897.

12. Hölzel, B. K., Carmody, J., Vangel, M., Congleton, C., Yerramsetti, S. M., Gard, T. & Lazar, S. W. (2011). Mindfulness practice leads to increases in regional brain gray matter density. Psychiatry Research: Neuroimaging, 191(1): 36-43. doi/10.1016/j.pscychresns.2010.08.006

13. Lagopoulos, J., Xu, J., Rasmussen, I., Vik, A., Malhi, G. S., Eliassen, C. F., Arntsen, I. E., Sæther, J. G., Hollup, S., Holen, A., Davanger, S. & Ellingsen, Ø. (2009). Increased Theta and Alpha EEG Activity During Nondirective Meditation. The Journal of Alternative and Complementary Medicine, 15(11): 1187-1192.

14. Aron, E. N. & Aron, A. (1979). The Transcendental Meditation program for the reduction of stress related conditions. Journal of Chronic Diseases and Therapeutic Research, 3(9): 11-21.

15. Sudsuang, R., Chentanez, V. & Veluvan, K. (1991). Effect of Buddhist Meditation on serum cortisol and total protein levels, blood pressure, pulse rate, lung volume and reaction time. Physiology-Behavior, 50(3): 543-548.

16. Talkovsky, A. M. & Lang, A. J. (2017). Meditation-based Approaches in the Treatment of PTSD PTSD Research Quarterly, 28(2): 1-3.

17. Kasantikul, D., Suttipan, C. & Worakul, P. (1986). Effect of meditation on mental health measured by center for epidemiological studies depression scale. Journal for Psychiatric Assessment of Thailand, 31177-190.

18. Ma, S. H. & Teasdale, J. D. (2004). Mindfulness-based cognitive therapy for depression: replication and exploration of differential relapse prevention effects. Journal of Consulting and Clinical Psychology, 72(1): 31-40.

19. Banquet, J.-P. & Sailhan, M. (1977). Quantified EEG spectral analysis of sleep and transcendental meditation. In D. Orme-Johnson and J. Farrow (Eds.), Scientific research on the Transcendental Meditation program Vol. 1 (pp. 182-186). Rheinweiler: Maharishi European Research University Press.

20. Woolfolk, R., Carr-Kaffeshan, L. & McNulty, T. F. (1976). Meditation training as a treatment for insomnia. Behavior Therapy, 7(3): 359-356.

21. Veehof, M. M., Oskam, M. J., Schreurs, K. M. & Bohlmeijer, E. T. (2011). Acceptance-based interventions for the treatment of chronic pain: A systematic review and meta-analysis. Pain, 152 533-542.

22. Meares, A. (1979). Meditation - psychological approach to cancer treatment. Practitioner, 222(1327): 119-122.

23. Cooper, M. J. & Aygen, M. M. (1979). A relaxation technique in the management of hypercholesterolemia. Journal of Human Stress, 5(4): 24-27.

24. Wilson, A., Honsberger, R., Chiu, J. & Novey, H. (1975). Transcendental meditation and asthma. Respiration, 32 74-80.

25. Chen, K. W., Berger, C. C., Manheimer, E., Forde, D., Magidson, J., Dachman, L. & Lejuez, C. W. (2012). Meditative Therapies for Reducing Anxiety: A Systematic Review and Meta-analysis of Randomized Controlled Trials. Depression and anxiety, 29(7): 545-562.

26. Khobragade, Y., Abas, A. B. L., Ankur, B. & Khobragade, S. (2016). Meditation as primary intervention strategy in prevention of cardiovascular diseases. International Journal of Research in Medical Sciences, 4(1): 12-21.

27. Wells, R. E., Burch, R., Paulsen, R. H., Wayne, P. M., Houle, T. T. & Loder, E. (2014). Meditation for Migraines: A Pilot

Randomized Controlled Trial. Headache: The Journal of Head and Face Pain, 54(9): 1484-1495.

28. Wallace, R. K., Dillbeck, M. C., Jacobe, E. & Harrington, B. (1982). The effects of the Transcendental Meditation and TM-Sidhi program on the aging process. International Journal of Neuroscience, 16(1): 53-58.

29. Beauchamp-Turner, D. L. & Levinson, D. M. (1992). Effects of meditation on stress, health and affect. Medical Psychother-apy: An International Journal, 5 123-131.

30. Smith, W. P., Compton, W. C. & West, W. B. (1995). Medita-tion as an adjunct to a happiness enhancement program. Journal of Clinical Psychology, 51 269-273.

31. Pupatana, S. & Sribundith, C. (1996). The effect of Dham-makāya meditation on personal virtues. Light of Peace, 8 8-10.

32. Nystul, M. S. & Garde, M. (1979). The self-concepts of regular transcendental meditators, dropout meditators, and non-medi-tators. The Journal of Psychology, 103(1): 15-18.

33. Taylor, D. N. (1995). Effects of a behavioral stress-manage-ment program on anxiety, mood, self-esteem, and T-cell count in HIV-positive men. Psychological Reports, 76 451-457.

34. Emavardhana, T. & Tori, C. D. (1997). Changes in self-concept, ego defense mechanisms and religiosity following seven-day Vipassana meditation retreats. Journal for the Scien-tific Study of Religion, 36(2): 194-206.

35. Sridevi, K. & Rao, P. V. K. (1998). Temporal effects of medita-tion and personality. Psychological Studies, 43(3): 95-105.

36. Nystul, M. S. & Garde, M. (1977). Comparison of self-concepts of Transcendental Meditators and non-meditators. Psychological Reports, 41(1): 303-306.

37. Turnball, M. J. & Norris, H. (1982). Effects of TM on self-identity indices & personality. British Journal of Psychology, 73(1): 57-68.

38. Alexander, C. N., Rainforth, M. V. & Gelderloos, P. (1991). Transcendental meditation, self-actualization, and psycholog-

ical health: a conceptual overview and statistical meta-analysis. Journal of Social Behavior and Personality, 6(5): 189-247.

39. Nidich, S., Seeman, W. & Dreskin, T. (1973). Influence of TM on a measure of self-actualization: a replication. Journal of Counseling Psychology, 20(6): 565-566.; Seeman, W., Nidich, S. & Banta, T. (1972). Influence of TM on a measure of self-actualization. Journal of Counseling Psychology, 19(3): 184-187.

40. Van den Berg, W. P. & Mulder, B. (1976). Psychological research on the effects of the transcendental meditation technique on several personality variables. Gedrag, Tijdschrift voor Psychologie, 4 206-218.

41. Mascaro, J. S., Rilling, J. K., Tenzin Negi, L. & Raison, C. L. (2013). Compassion meditation enhances empathic accuracy and related neural activity. Social Cognitive and Affective Neuroscience, 8(1): 48-55. doi/10.1093/scan/nss095

42. Shapiro, S. L., Schwartz, G. E. R. & Bonner, G. (1998). The effects of mindfulness-based stress reduction on medical and pre-medical students. Journal of Behavioral Medicine, 21 581-599.

43. Fennell, A. B., Benau, E. M. & Atchley, R. A. (2016). A single session of meditation reduces of physiological indices of anger in both experienced and novice meditators. Consciousness and Cognition, 40 54-66.

44. Kolsawalla, M. B. (1978). An experimental investigation into the effectiveness of some yogic variables as a mechanism of change in the value-attitude system. Journal of Indian Psychology, 1(1): 59-68.

45. Cowger, E. L. & Torrance, E. P. (1982). Further examination of the quality changes in creative functioning resulting from meditation (Zazen) training. Creative child and adult quarterly, 7(4): 211-217.

46. Weinberger, J., McLeods, C., Clelland, D. M., Santorelli, S. F. & Kabat-Zinn, J. (1990). Motivational change following a meditation-based stress reduction program for medical outpa-

tients." Uppsala, Sweden, June 28, 1990: Poster presented at the 1st International Congress of Behavioral Medicine.

47. Tloczynski, J. & Tantriella, M. (1998). A comparison of the effects of Zen breath meditation or relaxation on college adjustment. Psychologia: An International Journal of Psychology in the Orient, 41(1): 32-43.

48. Astin, J. A. (1997). Stress reduction through mindfulness meditation: effects on psychological symptomatology, sense of control and spiritual experiences. Psychotherapy and Psychosomatics, 66 97-106; Shapiro, S. L., Schwartz, G. E. R. & Bonner, G. (1998). The effects of mindfulness-based stress reduction on medical and pre-medical students. Journal of Behavioral Medicine, 21 581-599.

49. Hyland, T. (2017). McDonaldizing Spirituality: Mindfulness, Education, and Consumerism. Journal of Transformative Education, 15(4): 334-356.

50. Cranson, R. W., Orme-Johnson, D. W., Gackenbach, J., Dillbeck, M. C., Jones, C. H. & Alexander, C. N. (1991). Transcendental meditation and improved performance on intelligence-related measures: a longitudinal study. Personality and Individual Differences, 12(10): 1105-1116.

51. Abrams, A. I. (1977). Paired associate learning and recall. In D. Orme-Johnson and J. Farrow (Eds.), Scientific research on the Transcendental Meditation program Vol. 1 (pp. 377-398). Rheinweiler: Maharishi European Research University Press.

52. Napoli, M., Krech, P. R. & Holley, L. C. (2005). Mindfulness Training for Elementary School Students. Journal of Applied School Psychology, 21(1): 99-125.; Schonert-Reichl, K. A., Oberle, E., Lawlor, M. S., Abbott, D., Thomson, K., Oberlander, T. F. & Diamond, A. (2015). Enhancing cognitive and social–emotional development through a simple-to-administer mindfulness-based school program for elementary school children: A randomized controlled trial. Developmental Psychology, 51(1): 52-66.

53. Chang, J. & Hiebert, B. (1989). Relaxation procedures with children: a review. Medical Psychotherapy: An International Journal, 2 163-179.; Hall, P. D. (1999). The effect of meditation on the academic performance of African American college students. Journal of Black Studies, 29(3): 408-415.

54. Alexander, C. N., Langer, E. J., Newman, R. I., Chandler, H. M. & Davies, J. L. (1989). Transcendental meditation, mindfulness, and longevity: an experimental study with the elderly. Journal of Social Behavior and Personality, 6(5): 189-247.

55. Abrams, A. I. & Siegal, L. M. (1978). The transcendental meditation program and rehabilitation at Folsom state prison: a cross-validation study. Criminal Justice and Behavior, 5(1): 3-20.

56. Pruett, J. M., Nishimura, N. J. & Priest, R. (2007). The Role of Meditation in Addiction Recovery. Counseling and Values, 52(1): 71-84.

57. Shafil, M., Lavely, R. & Jaffe, R. (1975). Meditation and the prevention of alcohol abuse. American Journal of Psychiatry, 132(9): 942-945.

58. Hanley, C. & Spates, J. (1978). Transcendental meditation and social psychological attitudes. Journal of Psychology, 99(Part II): 121-127.

59. Hagelin, J. S., Rainforth, M. V., Cavanaugh, K. L. C., Alexander, C. N., Shatkin, S. F., Davies, J. L., Hughes, A. O., Ross, E. & Orme-Johnson, D. W. (1999). Effects of Group Practice of the Transcendental Meditation Program on Preventing Violent Crime in Washington, D.C.: Results of the National Demonstration Project, June-July 1993. Social Indicators Research, 47(2): 153-201. https://doi.org/10.1023/A:1006978911496

60. Orme-Johnson, D. W., Dillbeck, M. C. & Alexander, C. N. (2003). Preventing terrorism and international conflict: Effects of large assemblies of participants in the Transcendental Meditation and TM-Sidhi programs. Journal of Offender Rehabilitation, 36 283-302.

61. Davies, J. L. & Alexander, C. N. (2005). Alleviating political violence through reducing collective tension: Impact assessment analyses of the Lebanon war. Journal of Social Behavior and Personality, 17(1): 285-338.

62. Taylor, D. N. (1995). Effects of a behavioral stress-management program on anxiety, mood, self-esteem, and T-cell count in HIV-positive men. Psychological Reports, 76: 451-457.

8

OUR STORIES

PERSONAL ACCOUNTS FROM THE MEDITATION CENTER OF
ALABAMA

The healing power of meditation, for which this book is named, is never more evident than in the personal testimonies of our members. We are extremely grateful for their contributions to this book and hope that as you read the accounts of their experience with meditation, you will beencouraged to pursue your own meditation journey. May you gain wisdom and encouragement from their words.

DAVID ROBERTS: CIVIL ENGINEER

My civil engineering career gave me a strong background in solving problems with logic. But logic couldn't seem to solve the anxiety that has occurred throughout my life. Alcohol didn't work, either. I've also tried anti-depressants, but they were more of a crutch than a solution.

After reading several articles about the benefits of meditation, I decided to give it a try. I made some progress practicing on my own, but only after finding the Meditation Center of Alabamadid I understand what meditation really is.

For me, meditation is now a way of life. It helps me live my life in this present moment, insteadof living it regretting things in my past, and worrying about things in my future. This simple, yet elusive concept has been critical in reducing my anxiety. Learning to love and accept myself (and others) has been another powerful concept. I'm now on a journey with my fellow meditators at MCA. We have learned and grown so much together, without judging, and always with loving, kindness.

∼

ASHLEY: RN

A few years ago, I was lost. I moved to Mobile, Alabama, and I was spiritually lost, and then literally lost, finding my way around in a new city. This gave me a completely new perspective. I finally got the courage to come to meditation class. Since then it has been a huge self-transformation and self-growth journey, and eventually I became a regular member and volunteer at the center. I have an outlook on life that would not have thought possible for me only a few years ago, and I owe it to meditation. Then, I learned what unconditional self- love is. I was having the most difficult family situation of my life happening. I asked my dear friend, Nena, "What should I do?" Her answer was simple, yet so profound.

She said, "Keep showing loving kindness every day with no expectations, and keep meditating! And eventually, that energy will be received." I was skeptical, but did it. She was right!!! It took some time, but it was the beginning of a beautiful profound new perspective of my life. Thank you. I haven't stopped a day since. It showed me that instead of searching externally to solve my problems, instead, look within. We all have exactly what we need already inside us. "Knowing yourself is the beginning of all wisdom." Aristotle

D'VORA POWER

Age: 65

Q: What made you become interested in meditation?

A: I began my spiritual journey at 21, and the first strong message I received was "study to be quiet." At first, I thought this meant do not talk, and I do love to talk. At first, I was confused. Over the last 40 years, I have discovered many ways to study being quiet. By being quiet, my thoughts became clear. I was able to think better and discover the many benefits. Meditation has increased my listening skills, contemplation, and my attitude became kind. I became more patient as meditation led me to discover inner healing. This developed as I learned how to love and accept myself, leading me to love and accept others. I have been meditating for the past eleven years, and it has been very rewarding and healing. I have a greater inner peace as well as greater love and compassion.

Q: How has meditation and the Meditation Center of Alabama positively impacted your life?

A: Spiritually, meditation is transforming me. My desires are changing, and I am becoming more aware and able to truly be myself. Many layers of who I thought I was no longer seemed to apply to me. These layers are peeling away, and the "false" me, and I am seeing the real me. The person I always knew I was, but for some reason I hid or only allowed "some" to see.

A: Now I am content and happy to just be myself. Meditation has helped me, I believe, to find more truth, and authentic, eternal, lasting beliefs.

Q: How did you learn about the Meditation Center of Alabama?

A: I began to look for others who believed in meditation. I found the Center through a class at the University of South Alabama that was led by Dr. Nena Nimit.

RENÉE

Age: 59

Q: How did you learn about the Meditation Center of Alabama?

A: I heard about the Meditation Center of Alabama while serving on a jury. During the break, one of the other jury members told me about the Center. I was looking for a spiritual addition to my life when I discovered Buddhism. I meditate because it is an important part of my religious practice, but also because I enjoy it.

Q: How has meditation and the Meditation Center of Alabama positively impacted your life?

A: I have been meditating six years. I am a survivor of childhood abuse and rape, so, I carry a great deal of anger with me. I have also suffered from depression and insomnia. Meditation allows me to quiet my mind. It has provided me with a positive and proactive way to deal with the anger I carried inside of me for so many years.

DANIEL DAY: FULL-TIME ARTIST

Age: 38

Q: What made you become interested in meditation?

A: I began to get interested in meditation while taking medications for epilepsy. Pills do not always do a good job (not to mention the side effects) when taking them to relax the brain. A bit of studying seemed logical. Reading a few books, meditation became interesting. So, I tried, and it grew. I have learned a lot and knew there is more to learn.

Q: How did you learn about the Meditation Center of Alabama?

A: I heard about the Meditation Center of Alabama through a post on Facebook that caught my curiosity. Being that I have been studying on my own for a few years, having a place to go was wonderful to me.

Q: How has meditation and the Meditation Center of Alabama positively impacted your life?

A: The Meditation Center of Alabama has helped me in many countless ways.

Recently, I was running low on my anti-seizure medication and I had to stretch them out for a few days by halting my dose. I had seven seizures in one day. During the last seizure, my mother called out "MEDITATE!" I began chanting Om. I closed my eyes and calmly smiled. There I stayed, smiling. It brings me balance. Meditation is the medication. Many times, it has stopped a seizure from happening. Now it has brought me out of a seizure. I am doing something right.

Q: What do you think prevents people from meditating?

A: I think what stops people from meditating is ignorance, general fear of change, and the thought of loss of faith. One can pray and meditate. I would say to them, "Let us sit down. Close our eyes and breathe for a minute."

URSULA: SELF-EMPLOYED

Age: 64

Q: What made you become interested in meditation?

A: I became interested in meditation during my time at a stressful workplace. I started to feel my health and wellbeing was compromised. I wanted healing without drugs.

Q: How did you learn about the Meditation Center of Alabama?

A: I found the Meditation Center on the Meetup website while looking for yoga. I feel blessed to have found Lar and Nena; they have given me a different perspective in life. I can say now, I am content and happy in my being.

Q: How has meditation and the Meditation Center of Alabama positively impacted your life?

A: The Meditation Center has contributed to my inner wellbeing. I have been fortunate to receive the tools required to learn meditation, which I believe is a journey until my last breath.

Q: What do you think prevents people from meditating?

A: The unknown, laziness, wanting a quick fix of discomfort prevents us from meditating. To people hesitant to begin meditating you can say Nothing. You must find it; it will not find you.

MEGREZ: FITNESS INSTRUCTOR AND AUTHOR

Age: 33

Q: What made you become interested in meditation?

A: My first meditation experience was when I was seven, but I began to incorporate certain meditation techniques in my mid-20s to help cope with anxiety and depression. I would take classes and I have been part of groups in the past, but the true transformation did not occur until I began attending the Meditation Center of Alabama's weekly classes three years ago.

Q: How has meditation and the Meditation Center of Alabama positively impacted your life?

A: I was prone to anxiety and depression when I was younger, with history of self-love issues. Meditation has allowed me to separate the destructive narrative and find the stillness and beauty in my own mind. I do not attach meaning or emotion to everything that happens around myself anymore, and I am able to see the true suffering of others and have more compassion for myself and for others.

Q: What do you think prevents people from meditating?

A: A lot of people fear the quiet. What prevents people from meditating is the exact reason why they should meditate. The churning of the mind does not want to stop. Meditation shows the power in stillness and the beauty of a clean and still mind. However, I would tell them that they should try it in a loving and supportive setting and form a group. It is easier to form any habit when there is a good group supporting you.

~

LISA BULLARD: RETIRED TEACHER

Age: 51

Q: How did you learn about the Meditation Center of Alabama?

A: My best friend recommended the Meditation Center to me to help me deal with my insomnia, depression, anxiety, and pain

Q: What do you think prevents people from meditating?

A: People thinking that they must undergo a religious conversion to an Eastern religion can contribute to their resistance to try meditation; but I would say, give it a try for several sessions before you decide about its effects.

Q: How has meditation and the Meditation Center of Alabama positively impacted your life?

A: Meditation helps me to sleep and get back to sleep. I know how to center myself better.

~

MARSHA HODGES: ARTIST

Age: 61

Q: How did you learn about the Meditation Center of Alabama?

A: When working at USA about five years ago, I saw a notice for a lecture in the library. I have always been a spiritual being and wanted to learn from others. Meditation was already an area of interest, so this was an opportunity to learn a different technique.

A: Meditation helps me focus on what is important when life around me becomes chaotic. With meditation, I can find peace so I can move forward and be a light for others.

Q: What do you think prevents people from meditating?

A: Living chaotic lives keeps us from meditating. Being constantly busy, going and doing too many things, makes us forget what is important.

Q: What advice would you give to people who want to start meditating, but do not know how to start?

A: Give yourself time to meditate to find that peaceful place within yourself. It will make your life better mentally and physically.

~

LANNY: TWICE-ORDAINED MONK AND VOLUNTEER AT MEDITATION CENTER OF ALABAMA

Age: 67

Q: How did you learn about the Meditation Center of Alabama?

A: I ate in the restaurant and found the leaflet at the register. I asked and found out that the Center was right around the corner.

Q: What made you interested in meditation?

A: I am in the Twelve-step program. When I began to get involved, it did not take long to discover how much the dharma talks coincided with the spiritual journey I am on. As I continue to practice meditation, I discovered how important it is not only in my spiritual progress but also in my emotional and mental wellbeing. My practice has increased from 10-20 minutes to an hour every day. Also, being able to be taught by

Skype and in person by very compassionate and devoted monks has been invaluable. I have been meditating for about three years now at the Center.

FELICHER JONES: RETIRED RN

Age: 63

Q: How did you learn about the Meditation Center of Alabama?

A: The activities community board at the hospital where I worked.

Q: What made you interested in meditation?

A: I went to a workshop on meditation for health.

Q: How long have you meditated?

A: Eight years.

Q: What benefit or effect did meditation have on your life?

A: It cured my insomnia; I can relax and go to sleep using meditation techniques, and I have released a lot of my childhood trauma.

ANONYMOUS

"Meditation is painful in the beginning, but it bestows immortal bliss and supreme joy in the end." - Sivananda

A: Meditation is like a small seed, and with daily practice we cultivate that seed until it blossoms into a beautiful flower. Discipline, faith, and a deep sense of self-awareness over a long period of time are all paramount to the path of inner peace; and the ultimate truth, or non-fear, is fully worth every single breath committed to the practice.

Q: What advice would you give to people who want to start meditating, but do not know how to start?

A: To people who want to try meditation and just have not gotten around to it yet, I would say, "Surround yourself with positive people for the motivation to move forward and take the next step. Ask for the truth in your mind, and eventually you will discover it."

Q: How did you learn about the Meditation Center of Alabama?

A: I noticed the Meditation Center building as I traveled back and forth down Airport Boulevard often, and one day I stopped by to look at the sign on the front door for the weekly schedule. One day, I went in on a Wednesday evening, and I absolutely loved it! It was several months afterwards until I returned, but once I did, I began to visit several times a week, and I continued to do so until work prevented me from coming so often. When I do make it home from my job now, I always make it a point to go by for a visit and see everyone again. If I do move back home, I plan on becoming a regular with my meditation family once more. :)

Q: What benefit or effect did meditation have on your life?

A: Meditation is simply my undying light at the end of the tunnel. I have discovered more passion, empathy, calm, and love, among many other things, within myself. Mindfulness and the truth that comes from it makes life incredibly rich.

LISA HOLCOMB: INTERIOR DESIGN PRODUCTION

Age: 59

Q: What made you become interested in meditation?

A: I was in my 20s when I first started to meditate. I have continued off and on my entire adult life. Sometimes I am sporadic, sometimes not.

Q: What do you think prevents people from meditating?

A: Life is fast and we are busy. I think sometimes time and pressing issues keep us away from the cushion. To people who are thinking about trying meditation, I would say, "It is the best way to relax, get quiet on the inside, and get to know you! We don't really know the self like we should."

CINDY SCOTT: RETIRED ELEMENTARY TEACHER

Age: 72

Q: How did you learn about the Meditation Center of Alabama?

A: I met Lar Nimit through the Mobile International Festival, where she invited me to her house to participate in a meditation introduction session with a visiting monk. This was the very beginning of Lar realizing her dream of creating a Meditation Center.

Q: What advice would you give to people who want to start meditating, but do not know how to start?

A: Meditation, like any practice, takes commitment. The longer you go without meditating the easier the excuses come. Mindfulness requires commitment, and we all get lazy sometimes; just like physical exercise, you must keep at it. To people who are thinking of meditating but just have not started yet, I would tell them that meditation is just as vital to your wellbeing as physical exercise is to your body.

Q: How has meditation and the Meditation Center of Alabama positively impacted your life?

A: Meditation has been one of the two key elements in my return to health after a six-year journey in overcoming Multiple Myeloma (a rare cancer of the bone marrow). I had been going to the Meditation Center for several years before I was diagnosed.

On many occasions during the four and a half years of high-dose chemotherapy, including two stem cell transplants, it was through meditation that I could go into myself beyond the grasp of the cancer and chemotherapy to a place of mindfulness and peace. Through the most wonderful medical treatment on the planet for Multiple Myeloma, the University of Arkansas School for Medical Science Myeloma Institute, and meditation, I am in total remission, walk two miles a day, and enjoy every day as a blessing. Through continued meditation, I have a deeper perception of life all around me as my journey continues.

LAWRENCE: PROFESSIONAL MARINER

Age: 63

Q: What made you become interested in meditation?

A: I started meditating because it seemed like a good thing.

Q: What do you think prevents people from meditating?

A: Lack of understanding prevents a lot of people from meditating.

Q: What advice would you give to people who want to start meditating, but do not know how to start?

A: Just try it. You are most likely doing some type of meditation now, unknowingly. P.S. It is not a religion thing.

Q: How did you learn about the Meditation Center of Alabama?

A: It was pure luck that I learned about the Meditation Center.

Q: How has meditation and the Meditation Center of Alabama positively impacted your life?

A: The Meditation Center of Alabama has positively impacted my life by giving me awareness of another aspect of the beauty of life.

ANNELISE BRANTLEY: MIDDLE SCHOOL STUDENT

Age: 13

Q: How has meditation and the Meditation Center of Alabama positively impacted your life?

A: I have been going to the Meditation Center since I was nine years old, and it has changed my life in so many ways. Meditation has helped me when I was stressed at school. When I meditate, all the stress I am feeling just floats away. When I go to the Meditation Center and meditate, it gives me a chance to bond with my Mom, plus all the bonds and experiences I get when I meditate with other people at the Center. I feel like I make better decisions after I have meditated.

Q: What do you think prevents people from meditating?

A: A misunderstanding of how to do meditation keeps people from meditating. You do not just sit around and say, "Ooohhmmmm." So, I would say that the stereotypes prevent people from trying meditation.

Q: What advice would you give to people who want to start meditating, but do not know how to start?

A: You should not procrastinate, because you will never get started. Meditation is well worth the time you spend learning to do it and it is free and freeing. It really helps with stress.

JENNIFER: PSYCHOLOGIST

Age: 41

Q: What made you become interested in meditation?

A: When I started coming to the Meditation Center in 2013, my life was hectic. I was a single mom of four kids trying to work and finish college.

Q: What do you think prevents people from meditating?

A: I think the thing that stops most people from meditating is feeling like they do not have time to sit and think about nothing, or they do not think they will be able to be still long enough to meditate.

Q: How did you learn about the Meditation Center of Alabama?

A: A friend invited me to the Meditation Center. When I came and saw the kindness and generosity of the people at the Meditation Center, honestly, it began to restore my faith in humanity.

Q: How has meditation and the Meditation Center of Alabama positively impacted your life?

A: Three months after I started attending the Center's group meditations, my father died suddenly while with me at my home. My meditation practice was an enormous help to me while processing my grief over the loss of my father. Within two years, I lost a close friend, and two more family members, including my mother who died quickly and unexpectedly. The consistent loving kindness and dharma teachings from the Meditation Center of Alabama have sustained me through the sadness and grief from the losses of beloved people in my life.

I am truly grateful for the Meditation Center of Alabama and the Nimit family. They may never understand just how much their example has meant to me!

KRISTINE ALFORD: YOGA INSTRUCTOR AND VOLUNTEER

Q: What made you become interested in meditation?

A: I began practicing yoga and meditation when I was eighteen years old, and they have become a nonnegotiable part of my daily routine. Through these practices, I have learned how to listen more closely to my body and mind, and these skills have transferred from the mat into my daily life. As a result, I have been able to navigate mindfully through stressful situations, practice gratitude more frequently, and make decisions from a place of compassion (both for myself and for others). Learning how to turn inward through these practices has changed my life, and I am grateful to share these skills with others through teaching yoga.

'NAT': STUDENT & MEDITATION COACH

"There is no happiness greater than the peacefulness of the mind" - said, Buddha.

I came to understand this when I went to a 3-week Meditation Retreat in Thailand. On one beautiful morning while meditating on a porch, I felt wholeheartedly content and awake. There is nothing I ever wanted more than the present moment. And for this moment, I am completely whole.

I will never forget that experience. Meditation allows me to be still and know myself. The practice has taught me to simply sit with whatever arises whether it is my feelings, thoughts, or emotions, and allow everything to happen without any resistance nonjudgmentally.

This experience led me to become a volunteer at the Meditation Center of Alabama in 2019 where I got inspired by Dr. Nena Nimit, a child psychiatrist, and meditation trainer. She is one of the most selfless, and compassionate people I've ever met, a woman who dedicates all her life to helping people tirelessly day and night. Along with a lovely meditation community and wonderful support from MCA members, I have now become a certified mindfulness & meditation trainer. I help people find true inner peace in life, reduce stress and suffering. I hope to spread this ancient wisdom to the world and contribute to a world that is more whole and complete.

You have read some fantastic testimonials from people who have found the healing power of meditation in their lives. The testimonies you have read are stories of victory through depression, anxiety, insomnia, and other life stresses. Learning the simple meditation concepts has released its power to the result of lives that have forever changed. This chapter would not be complete without the testimonial you are about to read.

Forrest Neal Testimonial

I used to be someone who struggled with my mental health during the chaos of the modern world. I wanted to experience peace and happiness, but it seemed very much like those emotions were only temporary because of how quickly everything around me was changing. Eventually, I was prescribed medications to help with my inability to manage the stress and anxiety of modern living, but they seemed to create just as many problems as they solved. This was a cycle that I realized I was caught in and I needed a more natural solution because I could sense an endless dependency to the medications on the horizon. That is when I met Dr. Nena Nimit and Lar Nimit at the Meditation Center of Alabama and began experiencing the true peace and happiness in my life that I always wanted to have, without the need for prescription drugs.

Growing up, I was labeled as hyperactive and prescribed ADHD medications. It wasn't long before I was taken off of them because of their side effects which caused me to stay up all night and sleep during school. When I was 17, the prescriptions were recommended to me again and this time, it led to a much longer period in which they were used. This time, I began attaching value to the prescriptions because they were helping me to focus on my school work, which led to good grades, and a feeling of hope for my future. The problem arose when I would continuously get a bump up in dosage after every doctor's visit until I was taking some of the strongest medications multiple times a day. My life became so influenced by the prescriptions that when I didn't take them, I felt "off" and would crave the rush from taking the prescriptions. It was clear to me that this was happening, but my Psychiatrist at the time encouraged me that it was normal to be experiencing the difficulties that I was going through and I had no idea what to do for a solution.

Continuing this prescription drug use while beginning college, it became apparent to me that finding a natural alternative to the prescriptions was vitally important. It was at this time that I began to notice a craving for other consciousness altering substances which helped smooth out the discomfort of the declining effects hours after taking the medications. I experienced this craving all day every day for over a year before I broke down with the realization of how trapped I felt. The feeling of being trapped is what encouraged me to research and pursue all possible natural alternatives which eventually led me to the Meditation Center of Alabama where I met the great teachers Dr. Nena Nimit and Lar Nimit!

I knew after the first visit to the Meditation Center that it was a loving and supportive environment where I could be comforted while finding the solution to the issues I was facing. The Nimit's treated me like part of their family which led to my growing interest in developing my own meditation practice outside of the meditation classes! Their genuine belief in what they were sharing was so strong and their actions matched the beliefs they spoke about so much that it naturally caused members of the group to want to help them by volunteering at the meditation center. This grew my confidence in exploring meditation as a natural alternative to prescription drugs for the issues I was facing and eventually with my Psychiatrists help, I was able to transition completely into a meditation practice and away from prescription drugs. I was finally experiencing the true peace and happiness in my life that I always wanted and it seemed so life changing to me to be out of the trap that I was caught in that I just wanted to help other people who were going through similar struggles in their lives!

Currently, I am a writer for the Internationally Published Meditation Magazine and I interview meditation experts, celebrities, musicians, and professional athletes to share their wisdom about the practice of meditation to people around the world. It's also quite often that I'm invited to speak at schools in the US to college students about the benefits of a meditation practice while living in the modern world. Because of the help from Nena and Lar Nimit, I'm able to live a happy, peaceful, and meaningful life. I'm incredibly thankful for the help that they have provided me with, and every opportunity I get to help them, I take full advantage of! They really saved my life and I owe a lot to them.

9

CONCLUDING STATEMENTS,

BLESSINGS AND LOVING KINDNESS MEDITATION

JENNIFER BRANTLEY, M.S.

There is so much evidence put forth in this writing collaboration that supports the healing power of meditation. By this point in the book, we hope you have found information and encouragement that meditation will help you with whatever struggles you may face. We are also proud to have been able to produce for you such a rich reference of knowledge, outlining detailed instructions on how you can begin to meditate, what steps to take, and what methods to use to take you to the next level in your meditation practice. More than anything, the Meditation Center of Alabama wants you to know that your entire life can be better by meditating. Your health, your work, your social relationships, your romantic relationships, and your spiritual walk can all be improved through incorporating a daily meditation practice into your life.

One of the greatest benefits of meditation comes from meditating with others. This community or group meditation is called "sangha." We hope that during your quest for peace of mind through meditation practice you find your sangha. If you live close to the Mobile or Baldwin County, Alabama area, we would love to have you come meditate with us at the Meditation Center of Alabama. If you do not live close, we send you forth with blessings as you venture out to find your family of meditators to grow with in peace.

If your living situation or location does not permit you to find a group to meditate with, there are many online communities where you can receive teaching, and live meditation sessions where you can meditate together with meditators around the world. One online program designed to teach you to meditate in the quiet of your own home with access to a peace coach is Peace Revolution. Peace Revolution is a 42-day program with guided meditations and an online peace coach to teach and guide you, and to check in with as you get started on your journey to a healthy, consistent meditation lifestyle. Never feel like you must make your meditation journey alone.

If you are reading this book and are interested in serious study of meditation, we invite you to browse the references in the appendix of this book. The reference section details many books and helpful articles that will enhance your learning about meditation and its numerous benefits in many areas of our lives. Further readings are also suggested in each of the first four chapters of the book. We want the great wealth of information in this book to aid students (of life or of school) in their pursuit of knowledge of meditation and its many benefits. In this book we have provided numerous evidence-based and personal examples of how meditation has significant healing power over a great many maladies facing people in the world today, including:

Physiological problems such as Migraine Headaches, Insomnia, High Blood Pressure, Coronary artery disease, Cholesterol levels, Cancer, Stroke, Digestion problems, Longevity, Stress, and Epilepsy.

AND

Psychological and Social Problems such as Anger, Childhood sexual abuse, Self-loathing, Low self-esteem, PTSD, ADHD, Insomnia, Depression, Anxiety, Disappointment, Grief, and Addiction

If you suffer from any of the health problems listed above, the best gift that the Meditation Center of Alabama can offer is meditation and our loving kindness. We hope that you will use this book as a tool and refer to it as you progress through your own personal meditation journey. We wish to extend our loving kindness to you and to all the members who have come to our center, as well as to all the teaching monks and laypeople. We wish to extend our heartfelt gratitude to the authors, as well as all who have contributed to this book.

LOVING KINDNESS MEDITATION

As this book draws to a close, we ask you to settle in and make yourself comfortable wherever you are: Take a few deep breaths, breathing in love and healing, breathing out negativity and sickness, breathing in peace and light, breathing out frustration and confusion, breathing in hope and happiness, breathing out sadness and despair.

Draw your awareness away from the outside world and into the center of your body. Relax, and continue to breathe. Imagine a beautiful light at the center of your body with waves of loving kindness flowing from that light and washing over you as you sit in your most comfortable, peaceful place. As the waves bathe you in loving kindness, you may imagine someone you love, a family member or a friend or pet that is dear to you.

Bring the image of your dear family member or friend from your imagination, down into the center of your body. Hold the memory of them softly in the center of your body and let the waves of loving kindness flow and touch your loved one. Now, imagine your group that you are meditating with, or the family and friends that reside in the place wherever you are reading this. Let your waves of loving kindness flow from your center into and throughout the whole room where you are meditating, covering everyone and everything around you with the beautiful light from your center. Now, imagine your neighbors, in your neighborhood, let the loving kindness that you are generating from your center wash over your neighborhood. Imagine the city where you live. Let the waves of loving kindness from your center wash over the entire city, flowing out over your entire state, over the nation and continent, and finally imagine the loving kindness from your center covering the whole world.

We, at the Meditation Center of Alabama, humbly send our loving kindness to everyone who reads this book—may you be healthy, happy, and free from suffering. May you overcome any difficulties or obstacles you face with grace and ease. We send our loving kindness to everyone in the world, to all animals, plants, and marine life around us. We send our loving kindness towards all sentient beings earthly and heavenly. We ask that they be safe, healthy, and happy, and that they be free from harm and suffering.

May each reader be blessed, be safe, be happy, and have a long and prosperous meditation journey. The Meditation Center of Alabama rejoices in the merits of all who have taken the time to read this book. From our hearts we rejoice in your merits by saying the Pali word sadhū, which means "great job!" or "job well done."

We bow our heads and from our hearts say:

Sadhū

Sadhū

Sadhū!

ABOUT THE MEDITATION CENTER

The Meditation Center of Alabama (MCA) is a non-profit organization teaching the Middle Way Meditation, or Dhammakaya Meditation Method along with wisdom based on the Buddhist sutras. The headquarters of the Dhammakaya Foundation are located at the Dhammakaya Temple in Pathum Thani, Thailand.

The knowledge of Buddhist philosophy and meditation is universally applicable to all regardless of race, religion or ethnicity. Members of MCA have historically been from a largely Christian background, proving that the truths discovered by the Buddha are universally applicable to all in cultivating peace, harmony and love in the world. It is our belief that sustainable world peace will only be achieved when each individual person is able to find true inner peace.

MCA would like to deeply thank the great meditation masters, Phramongkolthepmuni, Abbot of Wat Paknam and founder of the Dhammakaya Tradition, Venerable Dhammajayo Bhikkhu, Abbot of the Dhammakaya Temple, Luang Phor Dattajeevo, Vice Abbot of the Dhammakaya Temple, Khun Yai Chand Khonnokyoong, founder of the Dhammakaya Temple, for their immeasurable loving kindness in passing down all the teachings and wisdom that we know today. Thank you to all the monks and lay staff at the Dhammakaya Foundation and their endless support for our mission of 'world peace through inner peace.'

MCA Website:

https://www.meditationcenteral.com

Book Website with guided meditations: www.powersofmeditation.com

IN HONOR OF
MR. ROBERT (BOB) MAWSON

Mr. Robert (Bob) Mawson, who became the first European ever certified to teach Dhammakāya meditation as a lay instructor. Mr. Mawson was instrumental in establishing the Meditation Center of Alabama in Mobile and was the first to offer weekly meditation classes. Mr. Mawson's tireless efforts allowed the Center to develop and grow a following of students and supporters that continues to flourish today.

Mr. Mawson received meditation teacher certification during a special ceremony performed at Wat Phra Dhammakāya in Pathum Thani, Thailand, on September 24, 1999. He was given the Pali name Dhammaputta, which means "son born within the Dhamma." He trained directly with the President and Vice President of the Dhammakāya Foundation, a non-governmental organization associated with the United Nations, whose work is solely committed to establishing peace on earth through the individual cultivation of mind through meditation. Robert went on to teach weekly meditation classes at the United Nations for many years and was ordained as a Buddhist monk in 2001 at the Wat Phra Dhammakāya temple. He studied Buddhist teachings and learned how monks live and work in their temples in Thailand.

Bob was a unique and fascinating individual. He was born in England and joined the British Army at the age of fifteen, rising in the ranks to become a nuclear arms specialist during the Cold War. He had several medical problems, including a congenital heart defect, so he was forced to end his career as a soldier when he was taken for open heart surgery. He was not willing to lead a sedentary life, so he started a new career in sales in Denmark and England. He worked in several countries including Thailand during the 1970s and early 1980s.

He met his wife Marcia at the United Nations in New York in 1983 (she had lived in Thailand for ten years). They married the next year and had twin sons. The boys' Thai nanny introduced Bob to a form of Thai meditation at the local Thai temple in Mt. Vernon, New York. Robert proved to be very adept and soon achieved a very deep level of meditation. Then they went to Thailand with their sons in 1990, as Marcia was reassigned to the UN regional economic and social commission for Asia and the Pacific in Bangkok. There, Robert studied the Dhammakāya style of meditation at the temple in Pathum Thani, north of Bangkok.

While in Bangkok, Robert held guided meditation classes for students from many nations and religions. He inspired Korean nuns, Muslims, Catholics, and other Christians. He had a personal connection with his students, and they grew to love him. His students appreciated how he could help them overcome anxiety and stress and find inner peace.

Robert, or Bob as most people called him, was proud of his evolution from a warrior to a peacemaker. He loved guiding students in meditation, and he became very close to many of his students. After his experience as a monk and meditation instructor, Robert was invited to guide a group of meditation students in Mobile, Alabama, in 2008. He led the meditation group once a week for many years and spent delightful one-week retreats with them in Alabama once a year. The loyal group in Mobile was very special for him. One of his most devoted students confided that he changed his manner of law enforcement because of meditation with Bob as his mentor.

Because of his heart problem, Bob was put on a list for a heart transplant and was blessed to receive the heart of a young woman in 2003. The new heart served him well for eleven years, and it was during that time that he was most engaged in teaching meditation and several other pursuits. By 2012 and 2013, it had become more difficult for him to travel, but his spirit never wanted to give up. By 2014, the rest of his systems (especially kidney and lungs) started to fail. When he was in the hospital in October and November of 2014, he was well taken care of by some of his dearest friends whom he met through the temple in Thailand, including former Buddhist monk Josh Jayintoh.

Robert "Dhammaputto" Mawson died peacefully on November 22, 2014, surrounded by his wife, two sons, and many friends from around the world. Josh led chanting throughout the last day when Bob was still breathing but not conscious. There were memorial services at the Mawson home in Hastings-on-Hudson, New York, where the very same monk who had originally taught Bob meditation led the chanting. We also had services at Thai temples in New Jersey, and a wonderful celebration at Wat Phra Dhammakāya and along the Chao Phraya River in Thailand. He had a wonderful send off from this life and we feel that his spirit is still with us.

ABOUT THE AUTHOR

Sivaporn Nimityongskul, known as Lar Nimit, has a bachelor's degree in Economics from Kasetsart University in Thailand and a master's degree in Economics from Western Michigan University. She is a certified public accountant and worked as the manager of the University of South Alabama Chemotherapy clinic. She has been running a local Thai restaurant, for over 20 years. Lar founded the Meditation Center of Alabama, a non-profit organization, in 2007 and has been involved in running all operations since then. She is a certified MSBR (Mindfulness Based Stress Reduction) meditation instructor. Lar has been a direct witness to the power of meditation in improving one's physical, spiritual, and mental well-being. She wishes to spread inner peace and happiness to all.

Phra Nicholas Thanissaro Ph.D.

Phra Nicholas Thanissaro is an Associate Fellow of Warwick Religions and Education Research Unit at the University of Warwick's Center for Education Studies and is currently reworking his PhD dissertation entitled 'Temple going Teens: The Religiosity and Identity of Buddhists growing up in Britain' for publication. A Buddhist monk affiliated with the Dhammakâya Foundation, he is also a qualified schoolteacher and MBTI practitioner. He is a Buddhist monk of UK origin. He has been a monk for twenty years and has over thirty years of meditation experience. He pioneered popular meditation courses in Europe since 1997 and has several TV guests spots, audio CD's, books, book translations and academic articles to his name. He is also a UK Complementary Medical Association qualified teacher of meditation.

The Venerable Dr. Phra Nicholas Thanissaro is a Buddhist monk of 24 years standing. With thirty years of meditation experience, he is a UK Complementary Medical Association qualified teacher of meditation. Affiliated with the Dhammakâya Foundation, he is also qualified as a schoolteacher and MBTI practitioner. As a scholar-practitioner, during his time as Associate Fellow at the University of Warwick, he published widely in peer-reviewed journals on the formation of Buddhist identity in teenagers and continues to research the appeal of meditation in the West. He currently lectures in 'Living Buddhism' and 'Religious Individuation' at Claremont School of Theology, California and Willamette University, Oregon and is finalizing his latest book for publication entitled *The Intuitive Buddhist*.

Cay Welsh Ph.D.

M. Cay Welsh, Ph.D. is a clinical psychologist and emeritus faculty with the Dept. of Psychology at the University of South Alabama. Dr. Welsh received her undergraduate degree in psychology from the University of South Alabama, her master's and doctoral degrees from the University of Alabama and her internship training at the University Of Tennessee Medical Center in Memphis. Prior to returning to USA, she was an Assistant Professor and director the

Psychology Clinic at Lamar University. She then returned to USA to become the director of the Psychology Training Clinic at USA for over 30 years. She has conducted numerous workshops, symposia and research presentations over the past 40 years. These workshops have been on a variety of clinical, health and sport psychology topics, including use of mindfulness techniques. She has practiced mindfulness for many years and has taught mindfulness to graduate students, to health care professionals and lay people. She has used mindfulness- based approaches with her clients and has presented numerous lectures on mindfulness research to the community. She believes the skills of meditation and mindfulness are important components of healthy emotional functioning.

Kent Welsh Ph.D.

D. Kent Welsh, Ph.D. is a clinical psychologist who practiced in Mobile for more than 35 years. Following graduation from Wichita State University, Dr. Welsh earned M.A. and Ph.D. degrees from the University of Alabama. He completed his clinical internship at the Veterans Administration Hospital in Tuscaloosa. Dr. Welsh worked in mental health centers in Memphis,

Tennessee and Selma, Alabama. While working in the Counseling Center at Lamar University, Dr. Welsh taught courses in states of consciousness and introductory psychology. He was adjunct instructor of psychology at the University of South Alabama and former director of the University Counseling Center. Dr. Welsh was trained in Transcendental Meditation in the early 1970's and was introduced to Dhammakaya Meditation in 2010. He has used mindfulness techniques in his own life and has taught mindfulness techniques within his psychotherapy practice. He has given numerous workshops and presentations related to clinical psychology, hypnosis and meditation to professional and lay audiences.

Serena Nimityongskul M.D.

Nena Nimit, M.D. is a Child & Adolescent Psychiatrist who has been meditating since a young age. She earned her bachelor's degree and Doctor of Medicine degree at the University of South Alabama. She went on to complete her adult psychiatry residency and Child & Adolescent Fellowship at the University of South Alabama. Dr. Nimityongskul underwent a 3 month residential program to become a Meditation Coach from the Middle Way Meditation Institute and became certified as a Mindfulness and Meditation Trainer from World Peace Initiative.

Dr. Nimityongskul is a co-founder of the Meditation Center of Alabama and the University of South Alabama Meditation club. She wishes to spread the knowledge of meditation and inner peace throughout the community. She believes that sustainable world peace is possible when each individual person finds their own inner peace.

Jennifer A. Brantley M.S.

Jennifer A. Brantley M.S. began practicing meditation with the Meditation Center of Alabama in 2013 and began Qigong as a physical meditation practice in 2019. She is a part-time psychology instructor for the University of South Alabama, where she earned her B.A. in Political Science and her M.S. in Psychology. She teaches courses focusing on Child, Adolescent, & Lifespan Development. Jennifer is currently pursuing her PH.D. in the Applied Psychology program at Southern Illinois University – Carbondale, where she currently serves as a teaching assistant for Peace Psychology and Psychology of Work and Play courses. She plans to pursue a joint career in academia and consulting as an Industrial Organizational Psychologist. Jennifer believes that meditation with the Meditation Center of Alabama contributed significantly to her healing and grief process after the successive loss of several family members. She is deeply grateful to Lar, Nena and the Nimityongskull family and the Meditation Center volunteers for their profound generosity and continued efforts to spread peace and light to their local and global community.

SPECIAL THANKS TO OUR TEACHERS & INSTRUCTORS

Phrakrubhanavides (Venerable Manikanto Bhikkhu)

Phrakrusotthidhammavides (Venerable Sotthijanyo Bhikkhu)

Venerable Monchai Saitanaporn, Ph.D.

Venerable Nicholas Thanissaro, Ph.D.

Venerable Thaniyo Bhikkhu, Ph.D.

Venerable Vichai Phunnadhammo

Venerable Prawed Varasayo

Venerable Boonchoo Ariyadhammo

Venerable Piya Piyawajako

Venerable Anuchit Tikkhaviro

Venerable Pisit Jittasutdho

Venerable Sander Khemmadhammo

Venerable Pasura Dantamano

Venerable Wanchalerm Lamyaipongsatorn

Venerable Klint Kunachawo

Venerable Saccadhiko Bhikkhu

Venerable Sophon Panyasopanoe

Venerable Michael Viradhammo

Robert Mawson

Dawn Barie, LCSW, MSW, M.A.

Ruben Mollij

River Thomson

Pollawat Nakalak

Kent Welsh, Ph.D.

Cay Welsh, Ph.D.

Rosie Wimonrat

Dora Preszeller

MCA Teaching Sangha

Thank you Pollawat Nakalak for organizing our instructor class schedule for many years.

Thank you to our co-hosts:

Megrez Mosher & Kudzu Aerial Yoga studio

Shoshana Treichel & Above and Beyond Yoga & Salt Therapy

Thank you to all our volunteers who have tirelessly dedicated their time and loving kindness to bring peace to the community. We greatly appreciate each and every one of you.

SPECIAL ACKNOWLEDGEMENT

IN REMEMBRANCE OF CRAIG LINDSEY

1957-2019

Craig Lindsey held a Bachelor's in Cultural Anthropology from the University of South Alabama, and a Master's in Applied Medical Anthropology from Georgia State University. He was well-versed and experienced in various traditions of meditation and mindfulness. He was a certified Dharma Representative of the Middle Way Meditation Institute, a certified Mindfulness teacher from the Koru Center for Mindfulness at Duke University, studied at the Hay House for Mindfulness in LA, trained under Abbot Roshi Joan Halifax (founder of the Upaya Zen Center in Santa Fe, NM), and received his first transmission of the five precepts from Venerable Thich Nhat Hanh at Magnolia Grove Monastery. Craig served as a volunteer at the Meditation Center of Alabama for the past ten years.

Craig dedicated his life to do good deeds. He has participated in countless hours of volunteer work and became a meditation instructor to spread peace throughout our community. We will always remember his cheerful smile and his pure heart. Rest in peace, Craig.

 "I have set my intent and focus to bring applied mindfulness through meditation to disadvantaged, disenfranchised and underserved emerging adults that have not had the opportunity to tap into the inner peace that exists in all of us."

— CRAIG LINDSEY

The scope of this book is wide, but the motivations of the contributing writers are personal. From personal testimony to the sharing of the history, technique, and practical benefits of meditation, each writer desires to reach out, support, and motivate every reader to find inner peace through practicing meditation.

Want to Publish Your Book?

We Can Help!

* Manuscript Editing

* Book Cover

* Book Formatting

*Illustrations

* Publishing through all major retailers
(Amazon, Kobo, B&N, Apple)

* Paperbacks & eBooks

* Blurb Writing

* Audio Books

* Choose Your Own Package

* Author Retains <u>ALL</u> rights

We're here to help!

"Everyone has a story to tell, only the courageous will find a way to get it told. Let my team and I help you become courageous!"

LAK**E**VIEW

PUBLICATIONS

www.LakeviewPublishers.com

Made in the USA
Columbia, SC
08 October 2021